CALIFORNIA'S MISSION REVIVAL

CALIFORNIA'S MISSION REVIVAL

by Karen J. Weitze

California Architecture and Architects, Number III

David Gebhard, editor

Hennessey & Ingalls, Inc., Los Angeles 1984

Library of Congress Cataloging in Publication
Weitze, Karen J., 1952-
    California's Mission Revival.
    (California architecture and architects; no. 3)
    Bibliography: p.
    Includes index.
    1. Architecture, Mission—California—Influence. 2. Architecture,
Modern—20th century—California. I. Title. II. Series.
NA730.C2W45 1984 720'.9794 83-22580
ISBN 0-912158-89-1

Manufactured in the United States of America.
Design & Typesetting by Graphics Two, Los Angeles

Published by
Hennessey & Ingalls, Inc.
1254 Santa Monica Mall
Santa Monica, California 90401

Cover: *concept* Kevin V. Bunker; *design* Graphics Two, Los Angeles

CALIFORNIA ARCHITECTURE AND ARCHITECTS David Gebhard, Editor
Number I; *The California Bungalow* by Robert Winter
Number II; *Exterior Decoration: Hollywood's Inside-out Houses* by John Chase
Number III; *California's Mission Revival* by Karen J. Weitze

For Edmund Frank Henry Morgenroth

Contents

Foreword

California architecture came of age with the Mission Revival. After more than a century during which successive immigrant groups imposed inherited building forms upon a land whose physical diversity encouraged cultural colonialism, the Californians discovered in the Franciscan missions a source for a distinctive regional style. Picturesque or melancholic, depending upon the mood or purpose of the observer, the missions became through literary, artistic, preservationist, and promotional agencies the major source in California's search for what Karen Weitze calls its "mythic past." In the missions could be found not only the most notable, but almost the only material remnant upon which legend could be constructed. In a remarkable replay of England's Gothic Revival, the builders of California's expanding commercial society seized upon the architecture of a monastic and pastoral life as the form for the hotels, railroad stations, business blocks, schools, and bungalows of a secular and rapidly urbanizing state.

Karen Weitze does not let her reader forget that the Mission Revival began in romantic protest and ended with cold calculations as to the cash value of the Franciscan ruins for tourism and tract development. This romantic revival, whose architectural symbolism was embraced with equal fervor by the American adherents of the English Arts and Crafts Movement and by the regional manufacturers of concrete, was bound to lend itself to paradox. Ironically, the immediate architectural stimulus of the Mission Revival is not to be found, as its name denotes, in the Franciscan ruins. Instead, as the author suggests, it can be traced directly to the design of Stanford University by eastern architects. The seed of the Mission Revival, however, was inextricably in California's Hispanic and religion-dominated past. Yet the style was not prominently utilized in ecclesiastical construction, but in schools and railroad stations, the latter the reigning regional symbol for materialism and public corruption. And though the missions did serve as centers for teaching, their architectural definition—shadowy arcades and massive, unbroken wall surfaces—was not easily adapted to long banks of windows, heating and sanitary installations, and asphalt playgrounds. The author underscores the doubts, as well as the hopes, with which the Mission Revivalists attempted to shape old forms to new functions and new materials. But in practice, the revivalists rarely exploited the tension and interest inherent in this ambivalent situation. Their productions were, on the whole, both bland and static, evoking neither a new nor an old affinity with California's romantic past.

This book and the series it distinguishes are themselves testimony to California's cultural maturation. As part of a continuing investigation of the past that framed the maturing process, the book considers architectural references sufficiently distant to appear romantic but recent enough to be understood. The Mission Revivalists, like each successive wave of California's immigrant builders, were culturally conservative but, at the same time not wanting to return to the actual conditions of their architectural prototypes. The revivalists differed, however, from the builders of the earlier Hispanic, American, and European immigrations in drawing from a relatively recent and materially primitive past at a time of swiftly changing technology. Consequently, the Mission Revivalists' application of the architectural components of the Franciscan missions to designs for modern use and material was not notably successful. A study of the Mission Revival confirms that the usefulness of the past is decisively determined by contemporary need and interpretation; the search for identity is always selective. In general, the task of correlating the building forms of Hispanic colonialism to late nineteenth-century American proved insurmountable. Although brief in time and limited in influence, the movement was significant for supplying the disparate Californians with the unifying architectural symbolism of their state's most endearing and enduring legend.

Harold Kirker
Los Angeles, 1982

Preface

Why Mission Revival? It seems an appropriate question to ask. A style so commonplace in older downtown areas—a style so often seen in buildings of forgetable design, the Mission Revival has retained only the barest patina of public indulgence. Certainly everyone recognizes a few Mission Revival buildings as delightfully eye-catching: the Mission Inn in Riverside, the A. K. Smiley Library in Redlands, the Santa Fe and Southern Pacific depots scattered statewide. And certainly many of us have our local favorites: for me, the Hotel Stockton and the First Christian Church in Winters. Yet, how does what we see today relate to the past? What did the Mission Revival mean in 1895? In 1910? Did the revival have meaning? And, if it did, is that meaning worth searching out?

In 1975, while working toward a doctoral degree, I participated in a two-quarter seminar at Stanford. Assigned the task of researching the ties between the design of Leland Stanford Junior University and the California missions, I began down the path that would lead me through the intricacies of the Mission Revival. By 1976 I had discovered that Stanford's resemblance to the historic missions was no accident. During the period of the university's founding and initial design, 1885-91, a new style was being born. And like most styles, it reflected not just the present moment, but also the years of changing attitudes that preceded it.

What followed was months of sifting through *California Architect and Building News, Architect and Engineer, American Architect and Building News, Architectural Record*—in fact, each and every available architectural journal that offered further clues. Key dates and events, as well as people and places, soon became road signs pointing back into the 1870s and forward into the 1920s. Here was a style of complex motivation, one that belied its later vernacular abuse. Next were many more dusty periodicals: *Craftsman, House and Garden,* and *House Beautiful* provided more insight into architectural debates; while *Harper's, Lippincott's, Atlantic Monthly, Land of Sunshine,* and *Overland Monthly* opened other vistas.

By late 1976 I understood that the Mission Revival had a story to tell, but that it was a story in many pieces. Journals had offered much, but promotional pamphlets, newspapers, and photographs offered even more. Without the excellent collections held by the Bancroft, the Huntington, UCLA Special Collections, the California Historical Society, the California State Library, and the Southwest Museum, as well as those of numerous public libraries, the story would have remained incomplete. I am especially grateful to the librarians of the Bancroft and the Huntington, who pulled pamphlet after pamphlet, day after day. During one day at the Huntington, I believe that we set a record: in over 100 degree weather, we looked at over 100 pamphlets.

Finally there came the writing. The very nature of the subject made it a difficult task. First, I unraveled the events of the 1870s and 1880s that set the stage. Then I scrutinized the early people and their involvement, looking at the first Mission Revival designs. Once this was done, I analyzed the different building types, asking and answering a series of questions: What had the Mission Revival meant for California schools, for the railroads, for real estate promoters? And then there were the really big issues: What had the Mission Revival meant for the American concrete industry? For the Arts and Crafts Movement? Was the style just another nineteenth-century revival, or, was it something more? Straddling two centuries, how did this puzzling revival fit into the American architectural scene?

Returning to the buildings themselves, I also had to ask why such a rich history had remained unattended. It was not just outside the knowledge of the public, but it was also outside the knowledge of the historical profession. And that brought me back to the story of the revival—it was a story found on paper. The early buildings were almost all gone. To see the transitional designs, one needed photographs, drawings, and plans. And what about the first Mission Revival architects? Having discovered who they were, I wanted to know what they looked like. And so I searched for portraits—to call the players back to the table, to bring the debators back to life.

By December 1977 I had completed the writing, submitting the project as my dissertation in the art history program at Stanford. During the next several years I worked for the California Office of Historic Preservation and then for the

California Department of Transportation. For both governmental agencies, I traveled widely, evaluating buildings from Eureka to El Centro. Either through field experience or survey files, I crossed paths with more and more Mission Revival. As I suspected, a pre-1900 encounter was unusual, but the 1905-10 surprises on quiet main streets and back roads were more common. Fort Bragg, Quincy, Lodi, Fresno, San Juan Capistrano—all had their Mission Revival gems.

And so, in 1980, I went back to the dissertation, combining the field work with the previous research. The story of the Mission Revival remains a story heavily dependent on documents—many of them rare. For this reason, I have noted the appropriate archival collections in the footnotes. Often I have grouped documentary notes in a single citation at the end of a paragraph for easier reading. Rather than include references to primary documents a second time, I have confined the bibliography to a chronological annotated listing of only those studies treating the history of the style. And finally, I have identified all photographic sources, and to the extent possible, noted those illustrated Mission Revival buildings that are no longer with us.

Karen J. Weitze
Sacramento, California
March 1981

The complete run of *Builder and Contractor*, beginning with the first issue of March 1893, has now come to light at the Architecture Library, University of California, Los Angeles. Misfiled and held in storage, this extremely rare journal had been presumed extant only in broken form, with no known copies surviving in any collection for the 1893-1916 period. Thanks go to George Casen and Lois Webb of the Office of Environmental Analysis, California Department of Transportation, District 7, Los Angeles, for alerting me to their discovery. Review of the *Builder and Contractor* for 1893-99 corroborates the information here presented. Further details focusing on clients, architects, contracts and terminology, however, will allow an explicit look at the earliest Mission Revival commissions hitherto not possible. I shall present my conclusions as an article in an appropriate professional journal in the immediate future.

Karen J. Weitze
Sacramento, California
August 1983

Acknowledgments

For their assistance I would like to thank Paul Turner, Suzanne Lewis, Lorenz Eitner, and Dwight Miller, Stanford University; Susan Rosenberg, formerly of Stanford University; Betsy Freiberger, Stanford Museum; Harold Kirker and David Gebhard, University of California, Santa Barbara; Norman Neuerberg, California State University, Dominguez Hills; Thomas Owen, Los Angeles Public Library; Richard Longstreth, Georgetown University, Washington, D.C.; Thomas Hines, University of California, Los Angeles; Joan Draper, University of Illinois at Chicago Circle; Elliot Evans, Society of California Pioneers, San Francisco; Edwin H. Carpenter and Virginia Renner, Huntington Library, San Marino; and Ruth Christianson, Southwest Museum, Highland Park.

I would also like to acknowledge the following institutions and organizations for their cooperation: newspaper archives, storage periodicals, and interlibrary loan, Stanford University; Library and Documents Collection, College of Environmental Design, and Bancroft Library, University of California, Berkeley; Special Collections, San Francisco Public Library, California Historical Society Library, and Society of California Pioneers, San Francisco; California State Library and Archives, California Office of Historic Preservation, and California Department of Transportation, Sacramento; Rare Books Division, Huntington Library, San Marino; Pasadena Public Library and Historical Society; Special Collections, University of California, Los Angeles; Riverside Public Library and Municipal Museum; Special Collections, University of California, Santa Barbara; McHenry Museum, Modesto; the Los Angeles *Times;* Avery Library, Columbia University; Nevada Historical Society, Reno; and Texas State Library, Austin.

Finally, I would like to recognize Stanford University and Arthur B. Clark for the fellowship grants that made the initial research and writing possible, and Harold Kirker for his support and encouragement. For assistance in photography, I am most especially grateful to fellow architectural historian John W. Snyder for his skillful copy work, to photographer John Palmer of Palmer Photo Lab for his film processing, and to photographer Ron Busselen of Busselen Photographers for an always-open studio door. And to close, let me thank my husband David E. Meischen, JoElyn Rose, and, again, John W. Snyder, for many hours of editing and proofreading.

CALIFORNIA'S MISSION REVIVAL

Chapter One

Mission Imagery Romanticized

Plymouth Rock was a state of mind.
So were the California Missions.

Charles Fletcher Lummis
The Spanish Pioneers, 1929

The architecture of California's eighteenth- and nineteenth-century missions reflected the state's frontier character. Unsettled terrain and remoteness from Mexico and Spain, as well as a poor supply of building materials, led to experimental workmanship and simplified design. The Franciscans built with locally made adobe bricks, bricks molded from a mixture of coastal clay and an aggregate—either straw or finely crushed rock. All California missions had in common solid, massive walls with buttressing; a large patio with a fountain or garden; broad, unadorned wall surfaces; wide projecting eaves; and low-pitched tile roofs. (Fig. 1-4) Other features were arcaded corridors, arches carried upon piers, curved pedimented gables, terraced bell-towers with lanterns, and pierced *campanarios* (bell walls). Although often said to charaterize mission architecture, these design elements were by no means used uniformly. Indeed, it was their diversity that captured the romantic mind of the late nineteenth century.

Following secularization in 1834, the missions degenerated rapidly. Commentaries on California of the 1840s, 50s, and 60s rarely paid homage to the once prominent Spanish outposts. When it occurred, mention of the missions was realistic: "A more desolate place cannot well be imagined. The old church is partially in ruins, and the adobe huts built for the Indians are roofless, and the walls tumbled about in shapeless piles. Not a tree or shrub is to be seen anywhere in the vicinity. The ground is bare, like an open road, save in front of the main building where carcasses and bones of cattle are scattered about, presenting a disgusting spectacle." Even as late as 1863, regional writer Bret Harte made similar comments about San Francisco's Mission Dolores: "its ragged senility contrasting with the smart spring sunshine, its two gouty pillars with the plaster dropping away like tattered bandages, its rayless windows, its crumbling entrances, and the leper spots on its whitewashed wall eating through the dark adobe." Others mirrored these sentiments.[1]

In the late 1860s, however, attitudes began to change. From this time forward, writers commented with increasingly romantic enthusiasm. Promotional journalists hired by the railroads and boards of trade included descriptive passages on the

1 Mission San Carlos de Borromeo, Carmel, 1771. (California Department of Transportation: 1945)

In 1771 Father Junípero Serra established Mission San Carlos de Borromeo in the Carmel River Valley, only a few miles from the Presidio in Monterey. The mission served as administrative headquarters for the expanding Franciscan system. Its asymmetrical towers, with prominent quatrefoil window, were details frequently displayed in the later Mission Revival.

missions that were important in setting the stage for the later revival. National and regional periodicals also focused on California's Spanish heritage. Initially it was the taste of the times—a fascination with the concepts of the sublime and picturesque—that drew writers to the missions.[2] Melancholic tales highlighted mission architecture, drawing upon the size, mass, and the shadow of the adobe structures for allusions to the sublime. But it was the popular picturesque that excited the public imagination. Certain qualities, including irregularity of outline and plan, jagged light patterns, and an almost whimsical variety of design elements, lent themselves easily to excessive sentimentality. By the late 1880s a new historicism created an even greater interest. Finally there came a climax: rampant promotionalism. Together, these four phases—the sublime, the picturesque, the historic, and the promotional—ushered in a renaissance of mission imagery that immediately preceded the Mission Revival.

2 Mission San Gabriel Arcángel, San Gabriel, 1771. (California Department of Transportation: 1945)

As the wealthiest mission in the network, Mission San Gabriel functioned as a military and agricultural center. The pueblo of Los Angeles was founded nearby. San Gabriel's massive buttresses, and particularly its oversized *campanario*, were also design elements adapted for a mission style.

3 Mission Santa Barbara, Santa Barbara, 1786. California Wheelmen, Good Roads Tour, 1912. (California Department of Transportation)

Father Fermín de Lasuén founded Mission Santa Barbara in 1786, just two years after the death of Father Serra. The stone church, erected in 1815-20, was one of the last major structures in the mission chain and was designed in high classical style. Santa Barbara often inspired writers and architects alike.

2

3

4

4 Arcade, Mission San Fernando Rey de España, San Fernando, 1797. (California Department of Transportation: 1945)

Completed in 1806, the adobe church and its related out-buildings provided appropriately picturesque imagery for visiting artists. The arcade of shallow, thick-set arches, as shown here, was an oft-chosen view for *Century, Harper's, Overland Monthly, Craftsman,* and others.

Guidebooks, periodicals, and promotional literature of the 1870s and 1880s illustrate observers' interpretations. The missions were vaguely envisioned as noble institutions. Emphasizing their heroic condition, authors penned exaggerated descriptions. Benjamin Truman, a California promotional writer of the 1870s, contrasted the wood-frame structures erected by the immigrants as "vainly struggling . . . for superior recognition among the weather-worn and ancient adobes." In describing Mission San Gabriel, Truman wrote of a "monarch monument . . . that old and rusty pile," paralleling the church with an "ancient temple." This particular pamphlet, *Semi-Tropical California,* circulated widely, foreshadowing the increased distribution of such literature in the early 1880s. In *Occidental Sketches,* published in 1881, Truman went on to draw an analogy between the "mound-like effect" of Mission San Carlos and the Syrian Mount Carmel, noting that the mission had a "vast, solid and dignified, bearing."[3]

Articles eulogizing the mission "piles" also appeared in national periodicals. For *Harper's* of December 1882, Henry Bishop described Mission San Luis Rey as a pile with "the heavy adobe walls and buttresses" resolving "themselves back into their original elements" of "mere earth heaps." In a fictional romance with a mission setting, J. G. Oakley led the characters into "full view of the long, white pile of buildings," opening their eyes to "the still, old white Mission . . . the quaint, half-barbarous architecture." For *Overland Monthly*, promoter Edwards Roberts delineated the city's mission as time-worn, with the "peaceful serenity of the pile . . . ever present." Roberts described Mission Santa Barbara again for the *London Art Journal* as "an admirably well-preserved pile of stone, brick, and adobe . . . clearly outlined against a green background of wooded hills."[4]

The concept of an architectural pile paralleled artists' and writers' admiration for the California landscape. Most authors depicted mission sites overlooking the sea, dominating the plains, or contrasting with the surrounding hills. All missions had a commanding view. Even the sky was portrayed as a backdrop: "over all broods an air of tranquillity [*sic*] under this southern sky very suggestive of the spirit of the old monks." A larger-than-life architecture set in an inspirational environment called to mind the sublime. As Truman had stated, each mission was "framed in a landscape unlikely to mar the thoughts which this stately ruin will inspire, as one looks upon its noble towers, its ruined, grass-grown stairs."[5]

Writers portrayed adobe walls, once unbroken and unadorned by lichens, as symbolic of strength and durability. "Upon nearing the ruins, the old walls look like an immense depot . . . large piles of dirt . . . of which, at one day or another since 1776, were manufactories, nunneries, workshops, dwelling houses, etc." Not only did such descriptions evoke an awesome architecture, but they also created a mythic past. *All About Santa Barbara* exemplified this mixture of description and sentiment: "To the east runs a pillared balcony, where you see the priests in their gray gowns walking too [*sic*] and fro . . . All is surrounded by an adobe wall, broken and thrown down in some places, but lofty and firm in others . . . the glories of the sanctuary are bedimmed with the dust and neglect of many years." The missions were not the majestic structures claimed, yet writers remained undaunted. In one instance, the grandeur of the mission courtyard was even compared to that of the Roman forums.[6]

Such imagery transformed the remnants of the missions into noteworthy ruins. In 1884 Agnes M. Manning assessed California's heritage: "Their [the padres'] plans were well laid, their ideas were sublime. Even in the ruins that remain we trace their far-reaching purpose." She described Mission San Carlos as "a

5 Henry Sandham, Mission San Luis Rey, *Century*, May 1883.

Mexican independence and subsequent secularization severely affected San Luis Rey. In the 1824-45 period the mission deteriorated, and in 1846 Governor Pico sold the entire establishment for less than $3,000. It was only in 1892-93 that the Franciscans—by then returned to ownership—began restoration efforts. Father J. J. O'Keefe led the campaign, publishing pamphlet literature that contributed to the growing enthusiasm of the first years of the Mission Revival.

picturesque mass of ruins, with wild birds flitting in and out through its arches." For the fullest effect, Manning tied the mission to its setting: "in a sunny landscape, with all nature in a mood of serenity, the storm of time and change has left its havoc on the Mission . . . the gray, dilapidated walls have fallen in all directions . . . an owl sits in an empty window, contemplating the decay about him." Sublime and picturesque interpretations began to meld into an amorphous sentimental whole. By 1881 even Longfellow was drawn to the missions: "A strange feeling of romance hovers about those old Spanish Missions of California, difficult to define and difficult to escape. They add much to the poetic atmosphere of the Pacific Coast."[7]

California's exoticism made it easy for visitors to fall in love with the West. An interest in Hispanic culture contributed to their sentiment, while the mission ruins offered the finishing romantic touch. Certainly newcomers cherished the lingering sense of another time and place. Yet again promoter Roberts commented, "In its shaded corners, the thick walls of their church sheltering them from the outside hurry of modern life, they are monks indeed isolated from the cares of the world, dwelling in peace and quiet, kind, sedate, and in this prosaic century, picturesque and interesting." Although mission architecture might have appeared "bare and crude," the allusion to the "olden days" was stronger than references to reality. "The whole life of the valley clustered around the Mission San Gabriel . . . The town was most picturesque, with the grand old Mission building, its adobe residences, its oranges and vines, and the admixture of races . . . all of whom led an equally careless and indolent life . . . It was a society of which the United States could produce no counterpart except in California."[8]

It was in the writings of Helen Hunt Jackson, however, that both the architecture of the missions, and the life style it represented, were permanently enshrined. Mrs. Jackson wrote several articles on California for *Century* in 1883 and 1884. Two of these, "Father Junipero and His Work" and "The Present Condition of the Mission Indians," were especially popular. Although the author intended her work to be a serious criticism of the way the Indians were treated in the West, her idealized and sympathetic characterization placed the mission Indians in the realm of the picturesque, along with their Mexican counterparts of the California ranchos. Mission architecture, still not well known nationally, was also treated as picturesque. The pencil and brush drawings accompanying Mrs. Jackson's articles often showed the missions in ruins. Vignettes of arcades and crumbling arches featured picturesque irregularity and rude detail. (Fig. 5-7) In "Father Junipero and His Work," Mrs. Jackson described Mission San Juan Capistrano in terms far surpassing what she actually could have seen: "The peace,

5

silence, and beauty of the spot are brooded over and dominated by the grand gray ruin, lifting the whole scene into an ineffable harmony. Wandering in room after room, court after court, through corridors with red-tiled roofs and hundreds of broad Roman arches, over fallen pillars, and through carved doorways, whose untrodden thresholds have sunk out of sight in summer grasses, one asks himself if he be indeed in America." In her prosaic glorification she noted further that the missions were "proofs of a spiritual enthusiasm and exaltation of self-sacrifice . . . rarely paralleled in the world's history."[9]

In 1884 Mrs. Jackson expanded her interpretation of mission imagery in *Ramona*. A lengthy novel concerned with the plight of the Mexicans and the Indians in an American culture, *Ramona* drew upon the earlier *Century* articles. Considered a major picturesque epic, the novel became one of the three most popular books in the United States during its first year. Initially, Californians panned *Ramona*, but as national acceptance increased, the novel became a huge success within the state. About 1887 a "Ramona promotion, of fantastic proportion," commenced in the region, with picture postcards "by the tens of thousands" and Ramona tours by the Southern Pacific and Santa Fe railways. Having made its appearance, Ramonana saturated the public during the following decades, in the process elevating *Ramona* to legendary status.[10]

Initially, however, promotionalism was not so important as the romantic vision of *Ramona* itself: "The Señora says the Missions were like palaces, and that there were thousands of Indians in every one of them; thousands and thousands, all working so happy and peaceful."[11] Mrs. Jackson's writings also contained other threads of romanticism necessary for a reinter-

6 Henry Sandham, Mission Santa Inés, *Century*, May 1883.

Mission Santa Inés, established in 1804, witnessed severe earthquake (1812) and fire (1824) damage prior to secularization in the 1830s. By the time of Helen Hunt Jackson's writings, and of Sandham's drawings, much of the mission was in disrepair—giving both Jackson and Sandham license in their interpretations.

7 Henry Sandham, Mission San Juan Bautista, *Century*, May 1883.

The fifteenth mission in the California network, San Juan Bautista was consecrated in 1797. Unlike many of the other Franciscan establishments, it survived the turbulence of 1834-35 rather well. From the early 1860s until the 1906 earthquake, the mission in fact operated as a convent and orphanage. As such, San Juan Bautista attracted Sandham and others, allowing them to vividly contrast the sublime arches with the picturesque groupings of nuns and children.

6

7

pretation of the missions. Up until this time, both the explication of the missions as sublime (1870s and 80s) and the subsequent analysis of them as picturesque (1880s) had focused on an imaginary mission culture. It was only with Mrs. Jackson's writings of 1883 and 1884 that specific characterizations of California mission architecture were widely published. The "grand and unique contour of the arches," "the simple yet effective lines of carving on pilaster and pillar," and "the symmetrical Moorish tower and dome" are all indications of another aspect of the picturesque that emphasized Spanish, Islamic, and Moorish architectural traditions.[12]

The missions had drawn upon an archetypal monastic, rather than Moorish, design. Yet there were various reasons for a nineteenth century "Moorish" identification. European paintings, travel accounts, and Oriental romances had helped to create a fashion for the exotic East.[13] In America pattern books featuring Islamic architecture surfaced sporadically, with articles addressing Moorish-Islamic culture published in *American Architect and Building News* in 1879. By the 1880s and 1890s Moorish, Spanish, and Islamic architecture peaked in popularity, accepted for commissions ranging from exposition halls to the pleasure palaces of the newly rich. (Fig. 8)

8 Pasadena Grand Opera House, Pasadena, 1889. (Pasadena Historical Society)

Erected as a belated by-product of the land boom, the Pasadena Grand Opera House fell into severe disrepair by late 1890. At that time inventor Thaddeus Lowe purchased the closed theater to function as headquarters for his business interests. Lowe had come to Pasadena in 1888 to retire. After only a few years he had begun to take on new ventures and then needed the space the opera house had to offer. Lowe renovated the interior for office use, keeping a portion of the structure as a theater. The Mt. Lowe Railway Company of 1891 became the primary tenant (as well as Lowe's claim to California noteriety). Curiously, the opera house was located near both the Santa Fe depot and the very early mission-style Hotel Green (1891).

Readers thirsted for accounts of foreign customs, for stories with Spanish settings, for references to such cultures within their midst. By the end of the decade, *Harper's, Lippincott's, Atlantic Monthly, Scribner's,* and *Cosmopolitan* all featured Spanish topics. Quite predictably, perhaps, articles on New Mexico, Texas, and California next appeared. *American Architect and Building News* also took up the theme. In the two years following the 1883 publication of "Father Junipero and His Work" in *Century,* the *News* featured articles on Mexico and Spain. The main series, written by Robert W. Gibson, referred to Spanish architecture as "Moorish" or "Moresque." Cloisters, towers, and patios figured heavily in Gibson's discussion, with the author deriving obvious pleasure from "enough plain wall-surface, and enough solid, heavy architecture . . . to satisfy the desire for stability." Like the writers treating California's missions, Gibson saw Spanish architecture as "full of romantic interest," deserving a "few moments' pondering by the modern traveller here upon their ruined scenes."[14]

The California missions were also linked to the Romanesque Revival. Henry Hobson Richardson's work of the 1870s and 1880s popularized a return to Romanesque form, with an emphasis on the massive architecture of Spanish precedent. Sylvester Baxter, author of many articles on Spanish architecture, used this stylistic term in describing the buildings of Mexico. Like *Moorish, Romanesque* became an adjective applied to the missions.[15] By early 1884 the writings of Helen Hunt Jackson, the Spanish picturesque, and the Moorish/Romanesque Revivals together ushered in the first article on a California mission to be published in a national professional journal.

In March *American Architect and Building News* included a brief essay on San Francisco's Mission Dolores. Although its author did not use the terms *Moorish* or *Moresque,* he did stress that the structure was an "old Spanish Church . . . one of the very few relics of the last century." The essay took note of the white, simple facade, the red tile roof, and the front bells, using the term *picturesque* in his text. This emphasis, while generally romantic, also related the missions to true Spanish architecture. Another national journal followed suit the same year. Writing for *Inland Architect and News Record,* I. K. Pond discussed Spain's past architecture as influential for the picturesque movement and for future design. Pond depicted such architecture as filled with an "atmosphere of the Orient," providing "beautiful hints of old Moorish times." Projecting its impact, Pond addressed American architects: "If a Spanish house were as satisfactory in its arrangements as it is in the stability of its construction, it might serve as a model." This statement proved prophetic, for Pond was to be among the first to link historic materials and construction techniques to structural and design innovations. At the decade's close, one writer proudly stated that Spain and her historic building traditions were no longer a "terra incognita."[16]

Even as artists, writers, and historians grew knowledgeable of Spanish precedent, they realized how very little was well understood. Romanticists had invented a legend, but as their nostalgia became a cultural phenomenon, historians called for accuracy. Edward Vischer, a California photographer of the 1870s, early attempted both written and pictorial documentation. In two publications Vischer set forth the missions, describing each in the terminology of the sublime and picturesque. Although still laced with romanticism, the photographer's work represented a fresh direction. In the early 1880s artists Henry Chapman Ford and Ariana Day were also drawn to historicism. In their attempts to delineate the missions accurately, Ford and Day relied upon manuscripts, descriptions, drawings, and photographs. Both artists not only saw the missions as picturesque ruins, but also as historical monuments in need of restoration—a shift in interpretation that foreshadowed the preservation drives of the late 1880s and 1890s.[17] (Fig. 9)

Once a proper history was established, writers again seized the opportunity to glorify the past, interweaving fact and fiction. In its broadest sense the mission period was linked with an "olden time." Charles Holder, in *All About Pasadena* of 1889,

9 Henry Chapman Ford, Mission San Carlos de Borromeo, 1883. (The Bancroft Library)

By the 1840s only a ruined shell remained of Mission San Carlos de Borromeo, and by the early 1850s the buildings stood roofless. Henry Chapman Ford drew upon the dissolving adobe walls of the outbuildings and a badly weathered stone church for his imagery. For it was not until 1884, after Ford's sketching trip, that Father Casanova began a campaign for reroofing and restoration. Casanova's work also generated published pamphlets, bolstering the romatic momentum that preceded the revival itself.

9

made such reference: "The most important and noticeable remnant of this olden time is the San Gabriel Mission." Holder tied the missions most vividly to this past period, summoning the "olden time" once more in his description of Mission San Luis Rey. "Like the other missions it is falling to decay; but in the good old times, with its out-buildings, it extended for nearly a mile and a half." James Steele, too, in *Old California Days*, insisted, "First, there is the old time of the Missions, part of the scheme of Spanish conquest, imparting a certain coloring which nothing more practical and modern will ever entirely wash out."[18]

An "olden time" acquired some clarity as writers drew an analogy between the colonial settlements of the East and those of the West. Mission architecture was the one outstanding reminder of California's claim to this early history, and it soon became a symbol of her antiquity. Since California's past was agrarian and Hispanic, it could be offered as the nobler model: "during the period in which the question of American independence was being agitated on the Altantic sea-board, there were at work on the Pacific Coast forces that were exerting all their power upon the development of the rich country, and the reclamation of its people from barbarism." The missionaries were seen as "the first colonists of Alta California." They were "those who . . . laid the foundation of our Pacific States." With this assessment came the realization that the missions were the "landmarks of its [California's] civilization." Mission San Diego's founding was even compared with the birth of the nation: "The present 'Old Mission' buildings . . . were commenced in the year 1776, and are . . . just the age of our American Republic."[19]

Within California the 1880s also fostered a genuine, scholarly focus. Manifested as written histories, state organizations, mission centennials and the beginnings of preservation efforts, this concentration added yet another thread to California's fascination with its past. Initially, factual histories were few. Picturesque, descriptive accounts were more readily received. Yet serious articles and books assumed a place in the literature as early as 1881, with historian John S. Hittell's article "California Under the Friars" published in *The Californian* in May. Francisco L. Ortega's *The Mission Churches of California* followed. Published in New York in 1882, it was one of the select detailed accounts of these years printed through an Eastern publishing house. Certainly, sporadic descriptions had been written for local journals before the 1880s, but it was in this decade that such articles were to attain more than random significance.

The movement towards historicism gained momentum through publicity surrounding the discovery of Father Junípero Serra's gravesite at Mission San Carlos de Borromeo in Carmel. As founder of the California missions, Father Serra was a prominent historic figure. In 1882 Father Casanova opened a campaign to stop vandalism, to record the life of Serra, to erect a monument over the grave, and to repair the mission buildings. San Francisco newspapers adopted the theme in earnest, noting the hitherto overlooked need for preservation.[20] At the close of the two-year drive for contributions, the "grim and gaunt . . . weather-beaten" church was reroofed. Then *California Architect and Building News* took up the cause, applauding the accuracy of the restoration. The November 1884 article signified the interest of California's architects.[21]

Between 1884 and 1886 Hubert Howe Bancraft also published a set of volumes on California. Illustrating the rapidly growing historical perspective, they provided a ready source for meticulously gathered information on the missions—facts gleaned from the mission records themselves. During this same period the California Historical Society was founded. By the decade's end books and articles providing a strict historical account of the California missions had joined the romantic literature. J. J. O'Keefe's slim volume of 1886 on Mission Santa Barbara, Ella Sterling Cummins's *Cosmopolitan* article of 1887, the Los Angeles *Times* mission series of 1888—all were indicative of the new historicism.[22]

In addition, the late 1880s heard repeated calls for preservation. William B. Tyler, in his *Old California Missions* of 1889, continued the cry: "The Missions are crumbling and decaying rapidly . . . within five years important repairs will have to be made, or before that time several of them will have crumbled entirely away." Another plea originated in *Drake's Magazine*: "Of the many Missions and 'stations' in Southern California, the minor ones are largely hopeless ruins, and even the more important have mostly fallen somewhat to decay. In only a few are pains being taken to preserve the noble edifices from the tireless tooth of Time."[23] California writer Charles Howard Shinn also emphasized the issue in an article for *Illustrated American* in 1890.[24]

In 1887-88 the great Southern California land rush provided yet another stimulus for the mission fascination. With the arrival of tourists and settlers, the historicism of the 1880s gave way to the promotionalism of the 1890s. More than one hundred "boom towns" were built in Los Angeles County between 1884 and 1888; 79,350 acres were laid out between January 1887 and July 1889 alone. Railroads, boards of trade, and chambers of commerce embarked upon a tremendous promotion, with Los Angeles distributing over two million pamphlets between 1888 and 1892. California's missions, as well as legendary sites taken from *Ramona*, became prime attractions. Tourists inquired about characters and places mentioned in Helen Hunt Jackson's writings, causing promoters to give ample pamphlet space to both "The Home of

Ramona" and the missions.[25]

The Los Angeles *Times* ran a large advertisement for the townsite of "Ramona" in 1886: "RAMONA! The Greatest Attraction Yet Offered. In the Way of Desirable Real Estate Investment and For Beautiful Villa Homes." Land speculators also exploited the public by using Spanish place-names and romance-laden descriptions: "The Boom at Alhambra! Don't be slow if you want a bargain in the most desirable spot in Southern California—In the LATTIN [*sic*] SUBDIVISION." In 1887 the Pacific Land Improvement Company advertised another boom town: "San-Juan-By-the-Sea! Near the Picturesque Ruins of the 'Old Mission of San Juan Capistrano.' "[26] Promoters went even further, arranging countless train trips to visit the missions and the "Home of Ramona." In Ventura County promoters adopted "Camulos," an inland site between Santa Barbara and Los Angeles, while in San Diego County they seized upon the Rancho Guajome near Oceanside. Railroad literature described the missions as "worthy a glance from the tourists [*sic*] eye," with the Southern Pacific, from 1888 to 1890, publishing numerous pamphlets that included sections on the missions.[27] Even the California Wheelmen got into the act. (Fig. 10) Bicycle enthusiasts, the Wheelmen campaigned for road improvements, highlighting Ramona's Home, the missions, and several Mission Revial buildings during its Good Roads Tours of 1912 and 1914.[28]

10 California Wheelmen, ''Home of Ramona,'' Good Roads Tour, 1914. (California Department of Transportation)

The California Good Roads Tour of 1914 reflected the past. A 'Pilot Tour of the *Pasear* (the traveled way),' the caravan of Studebakers visited each of the Franciscan missions, as well as the 'Home of Ramona' and the Mission Inn in Riverside. The tour itself was similar to many such guided trips that had been initiated with the publication of *Ramona* in 1884. Shown here was the Guajome Rancho adobe, located north of San Diego near Oceanside.

10

11 Charles Fletcher Lummis, c. 1889. (California State Library, Sacramento)

Historian Franklin Walker dubbed Charles Fletcher Lummis 'the impresario of the Southern California tourist renaissance.' But he was much more than that. Lummis certainly promoted the region intensely, yet he also led the mission preservation movement. Over a period of forty years he authored many articles and numerous volumes on the West and Southwest, focusing on Spanish and Indian culture.

More interesting, however, was the architectural image projected by popular literature of the time. The same qualities that had been cited previously as typically "mission" again surfaced in descriptions streamlined for the tourist. Thick whitewashed walls, quaint bell towers, red tile roofs, rows of fallen arches, and enclosed courtyards paraded before the reader. At this juncture, the desired effect was unabashedly promotional. "San Luis Rey was the richest of the missions of Alta California . . . the ruins are one of the objects of interest to tourists and artists." Many had become "smitten with . . . original romantic scenes." By 1887-88 *Ramona* was no longer fiction, while the steady publication of accurate mission literature became increasingly removed from the public mind.[29]

One of the chief figures involved with promotional efforts was Charles Fletcher Lummis, a flamboyant newspaper reporter from Cincinnati. Hired by the Los Angeles *Times*, Lummis published *The Home of Ramona* in 1888, thus beginning the mountain of literature that accrued to his name. In it he referred to *Ramona* as the *"Uncle Tom's Cabin* of the Indians." Lummis continued his writing with *The Old Missions*. In that piece he painted the familiar hazy, romantic picture that so enraptured the tourist: "Dreamy and dutiful daughter of sunny Spain . . . with neither regret for yesterday nor care for tomorrow, the Southern California of quarter of a century ago enjoyed its perennial siesta . . . Between its sleepy Spanish past and its sleepless American present, few links remain. Practically the sole staunch survivors of those old days of romance are the venerable Missions."[30] (Fig. 11)

From the outset rhetoric dominated all Lummis wrote. As Franklin Walker phrased it, "It remained for Charles Fletcher Lummis to make a real selling point of the Spanish past." In "The Old Missions," written for *Drake's Magazine* in 1889, Lummis attributed the heightened vogue of California's missions to the fortuitous combination of Helen Hunt Jackson, the missions, and *Ramona*: "The Missions of Southern California are touched with additional interest . . . several of them figured in . . . 'Ramona' . . . Her [Mrs. Jackson's] pen has made all these crumbling piles dearer and more beautiful." As early as 1895, Lummis shrewdly noted that the missions were the "best capital Southern California has." Repeatedly, in 1916, 1923, 1927, and 1929, he made statements about the economic role of romance. Each time he stressed the missions' historic presence over the assets of citrus farming, oil, and climate— acknowledging in 1916 the missions' preeminence as a model for the "architecture of modern California." In an interview with Frank Miller, owner of Riverside's Mission Inn, Lummis asked what *Ramona* had been worth in dollars and cents to California. Miller answered, "'I figure that book has brought at least fifty million dollars into this region.'" Charles Fletcher Lummis was probably most astute when he concluded, in 1929, "Plymouth Rock was a state of mind. So were the California Missions." It was a euphoric state that helped create the Mission Revival.[31]

Public enthusiasm also stimulated the advertising industry. One could buy "Pala peaches...a box of mission oranges, a 'Sonoma Mission lot,' or a home in St. Francis Woods." Even as early as 1895, such commercial by-lines as "Old Mission Hand Cut Olives" and "California Mission Eucalyptus Lozenges" sought the eyes of the community. (Fig. 12) Such imagery held the stage through a superficial appeal. Ironically the Catholic Church played virtually no role in the commotion, nor did a fascination with Spanish culture prompt schools to initiate a second-language program.[32]

In addition to the outright promotionalism, numerous publications also dispersed mission imagery during the tourist boom. William B. Tyler published his photographs as *Old California Missions* (1889) and *Old Missions—California* (1890).[33] Each folio vied with its successor as the most complete, most artistic, or most historic; by 1900 a representative group of books had appeared.[34] In Southern California, especially, there developed a nucleus of mission painters and etchers. *Land of Sunshine* reprinted Elmer Wachtel's etchings in many of its advertisements and layout designs. Alexander F. Harmer and H. Koch were among those actively exhibiting their watercolors, while Adam Clark Vroman, a documentary photographer and a close friend of Lummis's, visited and recorded all the missions between 1895 and 1905. Harmer even painted a much publicized watercolor series of Camulos. In 1897 Ernest Warburton Shurtleff, in *The Old Missions of California*, published in Boston, used color illustrations by Louis K. Harlow in combination with his own text for still another marketable book.[35]

12 "California Mission Eucalyptus Lozenges," *Land of Sunshine*, January 1897. (The Bancroft Library)
The California Eucalyptus Company capitalized on public sentiment when in 1897 they advertised one of their products: California Mission Eucalyptus Lozenges. San Luis Rey had little to do with cough and cold medicines, yet the mission became the product trademark.

Not surprisingly, major California artists soon were also involved. Henry Chapman Ford allowed his etchings to be associated with the tourist market. His earlier works appeared in one of Edwards Roberts's guidebooks, *Santa Barbara and Around There*, published in Boston in 1886. In that instance his interpretations served as the pictorial equivalent of Roberts's swollen text: "It does not seem as though we were in America or living in this century...It is Spain once more...near by...there must be the Alhambra...But it is America, and California, and better yet, it is the home of Ramona." *California Architect and Building News* further articulated Ford's role in the public arena in an announcement noting that the artist was preparing a set of mission watercolors for the 1893 Columbian Exposition in Chicago.[36]

Edwin Deakin and William Keith, too, contributed to the missionizing of California. By 1900 Deakin, a landscape painter, had completed three sets of the twenty-one missions, had published a folio of black and white reproductions, and had involved himself actively in preservation efforts. William Keith executed a group of mission sketches in 1883 and evidently painted several versions at a later date. Although little is known about this work, Keith was clearly associated with mission publicity. Charles Howard Shinn, in an 1890 article on the missions, commented, "from an artistic standpoint nothing better has been done than Edith Loring Pierce's etching of 'Old Carmel Mission' (San Carlos de Borromeo), after a painting of Keith's." Even if only secondhand, then, Keith's work reached the public.[37]

Certainly the sublime, picturesque, historic, and promotional aspects of mission interest overlapped during the 1870s and 1880s. Although these phases occurred in a rough chronological sequence, an occasional writer interpreted the missions as sublime as late as 1890, while someone else had commented on the missions' appeal for visitors as early as the 1870s. What was important, however, was the compounded momentum. From the neglect of mid-century to the notoriety of the pre-*Ramona* years—from the popular historicism of an olden time to the scholasticism and call for preservation, the California missions stimulated cycles of public fascination. In a very real sense, Americans' interest came full circle. With the promotionalism of the Southern California land rush of the late 1880s, the public found itself transfixed not with what had been, but with what might have been—a legend of the missions. In the end, facts of mission imagery were well mixed with fantasy, setting the stage for the revival that was yet to come.

Chapter Two

An Architecture of California

Study the character of the region . . . the type of . . . roof, balcony and ornament best adapted to its vicinage.

Susan Power, "Pacific Houses and Homes, I,"
Overland Monthly, October 1883

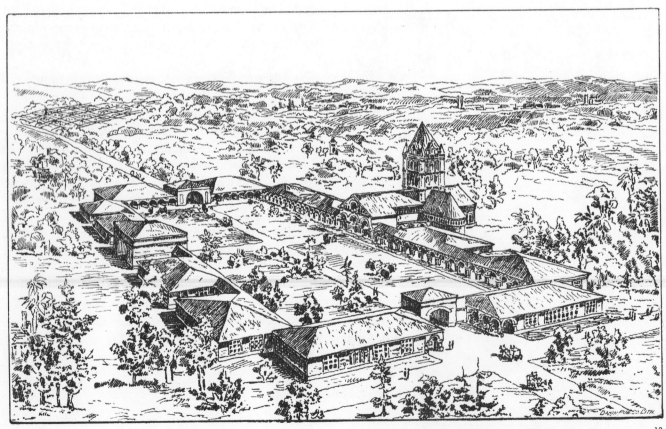

13

As early as 1878, an Eastern journalist had commented in *All About Santa Barbara*, "If I intended to live in Santa Barbara, I would domicile myself in an adobe house . . . Who would live in a structure of wood and brick if they could get a palace of mud? These adobes are to me most picturesque and comfortable. The walls are smooth and hard as rock, from two to three feet thick, which makes the nicest window-seats and deep doorways. The windows are large, the roof tiled, and a wide porch runs all around the low dwelling, and harmonizes with the whole nature of the landscape."[1] Although fascinated with the picturesque qualities of California's adobes, this writer realized that the remnants of Spanish settlement offered something more than the merely romantic. Previously, wealthy newcomers had shipped houses in sections around the Horn, transplanting the familiar to the unknown. Yet the mild climate and Western geography encouraged experimentation. Houses demanded little artifical protection from the environment. Heating and cooling were no longer major considerations. Like the houses of the Spanish pioneers, those of the recent immigrants could be optimally functional, and yet without a rigid plan. The low, rambling house with porch, veranda, and patio soon captured more than the romantic eye.

Promotional writers of the 1870s and 1880s tailored their literature to the needs and interests of their audience. The railroad companies, in particular, distributed numerous pamphlets to prospective Californians. Quite naturally, housing was a standard topic. Ludwig Salvator's *Eine Blume aus dem goldenen Lande oder Los Angeles (Flower of the Golden Land or Los Angeles)* was among the more widely circulated pamphlets and went beyond the usual attempt to merely sell California. Published first in 1878 and again in 1885, it focused sharply on architectural questions. Salvator specifically contrasted the American technological innovation of the balloon frame, most appropriate for the high percentage of wood construction throughout the U.S., with what he interpreted as Southern California's own distinctly appropriate innovation, adobe. "Likewise one is able to judge from external appearances whether the house is American or Californian. The former is constructed from wood, seldom from brick, the latter from

13 Ernest Peixotto, ''Stanford University,'' Carnall-Hopkins, *Souvenir of the Leland Stanford Junior University,* 1888. (The Huntington Library)

Published in an official university pamphlet, Peixotto's sketch of the campus quadrangle depicted an early plan. Here only one courtyard, with cross-axial emphasis, is shown. As the university design matured, an inner and outer arcaded quadrangle, each with courtyard, defined the final scheme.

unburnt brick made from clay and chopped straw (adobe)." He noted further that California houses were distinguished by their adaptation to the mild climate. "The adobe houses are built after an old Mexican type and, if they are not always beautiful, they still, however, deserve respect as comfortable and appropriate for the climate. They are one-story and are composed of only one row of rooms, even though the owner might be very wealthy. The roofs are either flat, made from asphalt mixed with coarse sand and fastened all around with narrow boards through which are carried small, usually wooden, drains; or the roof is made from hollow tile. Around the house run wide verandas, which are supported by wooden posts. All rooms have a door opening upon the veranda . . . inside the rooms are very simple, in many houses with bare clay floors which however are without exception extremely clean."[2]

The housing issue itself was less prominent in railway pamphlets. Occasionally, however, arguments similar to Salvator's did appear. In 1883 *A Southern California Paradise* concentrated on the subject. Promoter R. W. C. Farnsworth noted that although all styles were present in Southern California, "one kind of house . . . [is] . . . more popular than another in this locality . . . it is a one-story cottage with all rooms on one floor and massed around an entrance hall as a common center. Such houses are very convenient, as they obviate the necessity of climbing stairs . . . Verandas are frequently built on two or more sides of a house . . . 'The pleasantest part of a house is its veranda,' is a common expression in California."[3] The imported, two-story wood-frame house with intricate plan had already undergone change. A more informal architecture was on the rise.

Climate and geography were certainly factors in the early defense of the adobe. Susan Power, writing for *Overland Monthy* in 1883, commented, "the New Englander and the Northwest settler must build their houses with a view to winter or wintry weather full half the year . . . the citizen of Atlantic towns must pile story upon story in his mansion or apartment house to save the price of ground." She continued, "The totally different style of building and ornament required by the opposite climates opens a wide field to the American architect and artist." Here was a call for innovation—a call for a modern California architecture. Power suggested that one "study the character of the region . . . the type of . . . roof, balcony and ornament best adapted to its vicinage." Looking to the West, the author emphasized historic precedents: "the low walls, pierced for coolness, and the delicate fascination of color, which make the Moorish house [adobe] the paragon for warm climates. It does not take great gifts of taste to find styles of special fitness for Californian seasons of sunshine."[4]

During the mid- and late 1880s architect Samuel Newsom

also stressed the newness of the West. Newsom's eclectic designs were entirely his own, yet he too was caught up in the transition of the times. "We have succeeded thus in producing houses which suggest the Romanesque, the Eastlake, the Queen Anne and many other styles in a manner which is free from the restraint of hard and fast lines, and which satisfies the dictates of comfort, pleases the eye and is peculiarly graceful and peculiarly *Californian*." Design was moving away from the borrowed towards something Californian. As William Henry Bishop more whimsically noted in 1882, "One had been inclined to expect a good deal of novelty and picturesqueness from these towns of romantic Sans and Santas and Loses and Dels . . . Let us believe . . . that their pleasing designations will act as a subtle stimulus, and that all these communities will live up to their names with an artistic development which they never could have attained had they been simply Smithvilles and Jonesvilles."[5]

The first major design that deliberately drew upon the missions was that of the Leland Stanford Junior University. (Fig. 13) The Palo Alto campus marked a turning point in the architectural development of late nineteenth-century California. Leland Stanford, like his predecessors and contemporaries, was enthralled by the distinctive character of the West. He, however, took the crucial next step. In 1885 Stanford commissioned a group of buildings that he believed to be derived from native California architecture. By mid-1886 the Sacramento *Record-Union* had compared Palo Alto to Oxford, emphasizing the contrasting Spanish and English heritages. Palo Alto was identified as "peculiarly Californian." Another article described the proposed campus buildings as simulating historic adobe ranch houses.[6]

After Stanford hired landscape architect Frederick Law Olmsted and the Boston firm Shepley, Rutan and Coolidge in late 1886, the momentum surrounding the planning and design of the university increased. In November of that year, Olmsted cited climatic reasons for erecting buildings suitable to California, commenting on the state's similarity to Syria, Greece, Italy, and Spain. Immediately afterward, MIT President Francis Walker submitted his consultant report to Stanford. Walker described the projected campus as arcaded, with one-story buildings of rough, massive stone. Although neither Olmsted nor Walker specifically mentioned a Spanish-California prototype for their plans, newspapers soon discussed Stanford University as Californian in style. In April 1887 the San Francisco *Examiner* quoted Stanford: "When I suggested to Mr. Olmsted an adaptation of the adobe building of California, with some higher form of architecture, he was greatly pleased with the idea, and my Boston architects have skillfully carried out the idea, really creating for the first time an architecture distinctly Californian in character." Other articles appeared in issues of the San Francisco *Newsletter* and *Harper's Weekly* from December 1887 through October 1891, including color illustrations of the projected campus, with a description of the architecture as Spanish.[7]

Popular literature repeatedly associated the missions with the Romanesque, Spanish, Moorish, and Islamic styles. Thus, it is not surprising that Stanford chose Richardsonian Romanesque as that "higher form of architecture" to be incorporated in the campus design. A university pamphlet of 1888 is revealing: "The main group of edifices . . . will be in the Moorish style of architecture . . . A continuous colonnade, bearing a succession of true Roman arches, connects all the buildings of this main quadrangle on the inner side, and entirely surrounds the court . . . In adopting this peculiar style of grouping and construction, it was the desire of Senator Stanford to preserve as a local characteristic the style of architecture given to California in the churches and the mission buildings of the early missionary fathers."[8] Shepley, Rutan and Coolidge, working as the successor firm of Henry Hobson Richardson, altered Richardsonian Romanesque design to fit a building type representative of California, that of the missions.

14 Shepley, Rutan and Coolidge, Stanford University, Palo Alto, 1887-91. (K. J. Weitze: 1977)
For the inner quadrangle, Charles Coolidge applied Richardsonian Romanesque details to a heavily mission design. The one-story format set the stage for the rusticated masonry, grouped arches, and squat columns. Tile roof and arches carried the Spanish motif further still.

15 Stanford University, view. (J. W. Snyder: 1980)

16 Stanford University, Richardsonian Romanesque detail. (J. W. Snyder: 1980)
Numerous views of the Stanford arcades recalled those published of the California missions during the 1890s. Paired (or grouped) columns with foliated capitals remained a hallmark of many derivative Richardsonian Romanesque designs. At Stanford the detailed column sets contrasted vividly with the immediately adjacent rough-hewn sandstone.

14

15

16

Notable features of Stanford architecture derived from Richardson included fenestration, arch types, carved capitals, and polychrome ornamentations. (Fig. 14-16) Although none of these elements appeared in the historic Franciscan buildings, their use was congenial to a mission style. Other components of Richardsonian Romanesque were more than congenial—they were coincidental. Red tile roofing appeared in Richardson's architecture, in the missions, and at Stanford, but the sculptural tile used at Stanford more closely resembled mission tile. Stanford and its two antecedents also made use of massive walls. The university's sandstone, however, recalled not white-washed adobe, but Romanesque ashlar masonry. The third coincidental aspect was the dominant use of the arch. Stanford's contiguous placement of arches drew heavily upon mission precedent, while the individual arch type was distinctively Richardsonian.

It was the plan and general character of the buildings at Stanford that borrowed most profoundly from the missions. One-story buildings, arcaded, with overhanging eaves, were arranged around a gardened quadrangle (or patio). A multi-storied church imposed itself as the focal point. Although a rambling plan had been reordered with a dominant axial symmetry, the mission character of the university remained. Richardsonian Romanesque detail merely replaced that of the missions. During the early 1890s photographs of Stanford University appeared frequently in popular periodicals and pro-fessional journals. In 1897 *California Resorts* described the campus: "Out of affection for the quaint Moorish architecture of the early California missions, he [Stanford] adopted a style following it as closely as was possible."[9] Continued publicity of the campus helped to generate further "mission" designs.

Another aspect of the university also linked it to the missions: its function as a utopian, educational community. Initial plans included provisions for an entire town, while Leland Stanford expressed his hopes that the college would train men and women in practical vocations as well as the humanities. A philosophy parallel with that of the missionary fathers was evident. In 1892 Stanford wrote, "I think we should keep steadily before the students the fact that our aim is to fit men to realize the possibilities of humanity, in order that our graduates may in a measure become missionaries to spread correct ideas of civilization." He reiterated a mission theme on campus with his choice of names for dormitories and streets. All were Hispanic. For instance, dormitories were named Encina (live oak) and Roble Blanco (white oak). Stanford also chose a Spanish colonization subject for the frieze on the university's Memorial Arch. Even *Century's* editorial department recognized the unusual nature of the completed design, writing Olmsted in December 1890 to request an essay on Stanford University and its relation to the "architecture of the Spanish Missions."[10]

Other buildings of transitional type appeared in the late 1880s, although none were to have the effect of Stanford University. One of the first was the Ponce de Leon Hotel in St. Augustine, Florida, designed in 1886-88 by Carrere and Hastings. The hotel incorporated a general Spanish design, adapted to the warm climate. Louis C. Tiffany was responsible for the interior glasswork, while Bernard Maybeck was hired as one of the draftsmen. Maybeck, then a young architect, later became one of the foremost members of the California avant-garde. The Ponce de Leon readily captured public imagination. Its covered arcades, patio, balconies, towers, tile roof, and garden fountain labeled it "Spanish Renaissance." In reality it recalled a more eclectic feeling for the Spanish picturesque. Carrere and Hastings designed one other Spanish-style hotel in St. Augustine, the Alcazar of 1888.[11] (Fig. 17) With the exception of a possible effect on Bernard Maybeck, though, it is unlikely that these designs influenced California work. Still, they did demonstrate the national fascination for Spanish architecture and the fertile possibilities it presented for Florida, California, and the American Southwest.

17 Carrere and Hastings, Alcazar Hotel, St. Augustine, Florida, 1888. Perspective published in *American Architect and Building News*, August 1888.

John Mervin Carrere and Thomas Hastings entered into partnership in 1884 after a brief period as draftsmen for McKim, Mead and White. Successful from the first, Carrere and Hastings immediately landed a substantial commission from industrialist Henry M. Flager for the Ponce de Leon and Alcazar Hotels in St. Augustine, Florida. The firm then moved to St. Augustine for a two-year period to supervise construction. Both men were under thirty at the time of the hotels' completion.

In California the 1887-89 years provided a special set of circumstances that would shape events to come. The 1887-88 Southern California boom and bust cycle not only reflected the wealth of hyperbole associated with real estate promotion, but also the general economic instability on the Coast. For the building trades, a severe depression had begun in 1886. During the next five years work was scarce, with the forecasted growth in Los Angeles and San Diego attracting a number of San Francisco architects.[12] B. McDougall and Son, Willis Polk, John Galen Howard, William P. Moore, Ernest Coxhead, John C. Pelton, W. J. Cuthbertson, and Joseph Cather Newsom all journeyed south.[13] Not surprisingly, they met with little success and stayed only briefly. Yet the experience did offer an immediate exposure to California's Spanish heritage—to the impressive Southern California missions. With business down, these architects also had the opportunity to sketch and to observe. For some, it was a time of idealized design; for the profession, it was a time that would germinate the Mission Revival.

Two of these architects, Willis Polk and John Galen Howard, especially lent to the momentum towards the Mission Revival. (Fig. 18-19) During 1887-88 both were living in Los Angeles. Polk was 20, Howard 23. While in Los Angeles, Howard went on sketching trips to the nearby missions; Polk apparently did the same even before the men became acquainted. Both men had migrated West in the 1880s—both had been influenced by the work of H. H. Richardson. Howard, in fact, had come from

18 Willis Polk, c. 1911. (California State Library, Sacramento)

Willis Polk began his architectural career while in his early teens. During the 1880s, the Polk family moved to San Francisco, where Willis worked with his father, Willis Webb Polk. In the years that followed the younger Polk gained more independent experience through other local and national firms. Polk acted as the Northern California spokesman and theoretician for the Mission Revival, 1890-93.

19 John Galen Howard, 1890. (The Bancroft Library)

After studying at MIT and the Ecole des Beaux Arts, John Galen Howard first worked as a draftsman for Henry Hobson Richardson and Shepley, Rutan and Coolidge in Boston. During the late 1880s, he traveled to California, where he stayed for several years before returning East. In 1900 Phoebe Hearst retained him in the planning and design of the University of California at Berkeley.

18

19

Boston, where he had worked in the office of Shepley, Rutan and Coolidge. Employed with the firm at the time of the Stanford commission, he had arrived in California hoping to take charge of a San Francisco branch office. When the position did not materialize, Howard moved on to Los Angeles. A focus on mission architecture emerged in an 1887 drawing by Polk and in a group of 1887-88 sketches by Howard. [14]

Willis Polk's drawing, "An Imaginary Church of Southern California Type," (Fig. 20) was not derived from any one mission. [15] Those which he studied likely included San Gabriel, Santa Barbara, San Juan Capistrano, and San Fernando Rey. San Gabriel's distinctive buttressing is present in Polk's design, while the facade is adorned with classical pilasters recalling Mission Santa Barbara. What is most striking about Polk's design, however, is its similarity to published 1887-88 drawings for the Stanford University church. (Fig. 21) The tower in his imaginary mission church is related to that of the Stanford church in design and location. No mission ever had a tower of this type, nor one so placed in relation to the church nave. In addition, the side chapel of the Stanford church is repeated in Polk's design. Richardsonian Romanesque details articulate both the imaginary mission and Stanford churches. Finally, arcading accents both. Polk, like Stanford, was helping to establish a pattern—one combining mission design with an accepted Richardsonian Romanesque. *Architecture and Building* published "An Imaginary Church of Southern California Type" in 1890. [16]

John Galen Howard's sketches and letters from 1887-88 also provide insights. Included in a sketchbook are penciled drawings of Richardsonian Romanesque buildings and their details. Present also are sketches of Missions San Gabriel, San Fernando Rey, San Juan Capistrano, and Santa Barbara, as well as several more sketches of Los Angeles adobes. [17] (Fig. 22) In letters from this period, Howard described the missions and adobes as of interest to architects. "I saw for the first

20 Willis Polk, "An Imaginary Mission Church of Southern California Type," *Architecture and Building*, April 19, 1890. (Documents Collection, College of Environmental Design, University of California, Berkeley.)

Polk's 'Imaginary Mission Church' was published for an architectural audience well removed from the California scene. Printed in New York, *Architecture and Building* likely did not circulate well outside the East and Middle West. Thus, Polk's design may not have reached many for whom it was most appropriate. Nonetheless, its inclusion in a nonregional professional journal did accomplish several things. Polk's design illustrated the focus of Western architects, and, simultaneously, it foreshadowed events to come.

21 Charles Coolidge, Stanford University Church, detail, *San Francisco Newsletter and Advertiser*, December 24, 1887. (California State Library, Sacramento)

Inspired by Notre-Dame la Grande in Poitiers and Richardson's own Trinity Church in Boston (1873), Coolidge's first design for Stanford University Church survives only secondhand. By 1888 the architect changed the detailing, and by 1898-1902 the design of the church—still not constructed—fell to another architect, Clinton Day.

22 John Galen Howard, "Mission Santa Barbara," c.1887-88 (The Bancroft Library)

Like other architects, John Galen Howard sketched the California missions. Santa Barbara had never fallen into a true state of ruin. Thus, the mission's monumental facade with extending arcades attracted architects because of its very completeness, its full presentation of a historic image.

20

21

time . . . a roof of the genuine old Spanish tile, —the very name of which is enough to make an architect's heart glow . . . a long, low, rambling pile of building of sturdy walls and naive distribution of voids and solids, once whitened but now stained and enriched . . . Behold the mission!"[18] One particular sketch stands out as analogous to Polk's "An Imaginary Mission Church of Southern California Type." Unlike any of the other drawings, this one was given a title. "Sketch for Adobe House," penciled and undated, included both plan and elevation. (Fig. 23) The design was more closely tied to Richardsonian Romanesque than to the California adobes. Tile roof and arcade are the only details associated with the latter. Like both the Stanford University buildings and the imaginary church design by Polk, Howard's attempt to create an architecture based on native California forms relied on the established traditions.

The late 1880s constituted a fertile period for architectural innovation. Between 1888 and 1891 Samuel Newsom published several illustrative designs. (Fig. 24) *California Architect and Building News* featured "Tia Juana" in December 1888. The

22

In the sketches, the following room labels appear: Bed, Library, Sitting Room, Hall, Dining Room, Service etc, Kitchen

Sketch for Adobe House

23 John Galen Howard, ''Sketch for Adobe House,''
c. 1887-88. (The Bancroft Library)
Adapting Richardsonian Romanesque form to the
unpretentious adobe, Howard dignified a regional architectural type, the Spanish ranch house. Squat, low
structural massing, punctuated by the closure of the
lateral towers, transformed a rambling composition into
one more highly architectonic. Rooms were disassem-
bled into a more nearly linear arrangement appropriate to the historic model.

design was Spanish in name only, yet the architect's flourish was notable. In early 1889 Newsom published three more designs: "Alhambra Cottage," "Precita," and "Rio Dell Cottage." All followed the precedent of "Tia Juana," deriving their association with Spanish architecture through figurative designation. Each was for a two-story, wood-frame house of typical late nineteenth-century style. Later that same year Newsom published a final design, untitled. (Fig. 25) Distinguished by the Moorish horseshoe arch, it came closer to a Spanish residential style. In 1891 the architect presented "Un Chateau en Espagne: Our Governor's House at Sacramento, California." (Fig. 26) A "French" chateau with Richardsonian Romanesque entryway, the large-scale residence reflected the publicity surrounding Stanford University. Fenestration and unit massing resembled that at the Palo Alto campus. Newsom's design also incorporated two elements of the missions. Inscribed "To be built of red stone. Spanish tile roof," the design referenced not only mission roof tile, but also a red stone fabric recalling adobe.[19]

With the opening of the next decade, Mission Revival theory and design advanced rapidly, becoming established first in Northern California. In November 1890 John Galen Howard, Ernest A. Coxhead, Redmore Ray, and Willis Polk edited the first issue of *Architectural News*. The architects had worked together in Los Angeles during the late 1880s. Now in San Francisco, they collaborated on a short run of articles assessing the missions. Although of brief span, the journal marked another phase of interest in an architecture of California. The announced purpose of the mission series was to "enhance the value of

24 Samuel Newsom, undated. (Security Pacific National Bank Photograph Collection, Los Angeles Public Library)

Born in Canada, Samuel Newsom immigrated to the San Francisco Bay Area with his family in 1861. By 1873 his brothers, John J. and Thomas D., employed him as a draftsman in their office. During the next decade Samuel worked in partnership with yet another brother, J. Cather Newsom. From c. 1890 until 1908-10, the Newsom brothers took an active role in the Mission Revival, both in partnership and independently.

25 Samuel Newsom, untitled elevation published in *California Architect and Building News*, November 1889.

Appearing only a year in advance of initial discussions for the California Building, the late 1889 Newsom residential design incorporated an emphatic Moorish horseshoe arch. Extensive porches on three sides of the structure denoted not only the 'outdoor' lifestyle of Californians, but also the evolution towards an innovative house type, with a correspondingly new style.

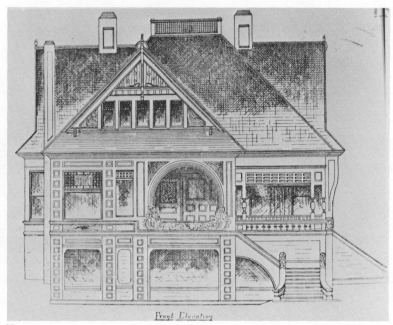

Front Elevation

24

25

TO · BE · BUILT · OF · RED · STONE · SPANISH · TILE · ROOF · PLOT · PLAN

+ UN · CHATEAU · EN · ESPAGNE +
OUR · NEW · GOVERNOR'S · HOUSE
AT · SACRAMENTO · CALIFORNIA
BY · SAMEUL · NEWSOM · ARCHITECT
+ SAN · FRANCISCO · CALIFORN +

26

S.F. SKETCH · CLVB · COMPETITION ::
FESTIVAL · ARCH ::: BY · "GVESS · AGAIN ::

SKETCH · CLVB · OF · SAN · FRANCISCO ·   FIRST · PLACE ·
AN · ADOBE · MISSION · CHVRCH ·   R · M · TVRNER ·

27

26 Samuel Newsom, ''Un Chateau en Espagne,'' elevation and plan published in *California Architect and Building News,* February 1891.

By 1891 debate over a California style had entrenched itself in at least San Francisco architectural circles. Always a creative designer and salesman, Samuel Newsom presented his idea for a new governor's mansion: a 'French' chateau with 'Spanish' details. Combining the Richardsonian Romanesque entry and fenestrated facade with the turrets and mansard of the chateau style popular in large-scale hotels of this period, Newsom achieved an eclectic height. 'Redstone' [sandstone?], as well as 'Spanish tile roof' would have given the mansion a finished appearance of an adobe Stanford. The residence never graced Sacramento.

27 R. M. Turner, ''An Adobe Mission Church,'' *Architectural News,* November 1890.

28 Presidio Church, Monterey, 1777. California Wheelmen, Good Roads Tour, 1912. (California Department of Transportation)

Appearing in late 1890, R. M. Turner's sketch of an adobe mission church took first prize in a San Francisco Sketch Club competition. Turner adapted the facade of the presidio church at Monterey for his design.

28

the same by paying particular attention to characteristics of special interest to architects, feeling, too that these papers will be both timely and useful in the proposition to represent this semi-Spanish Renaissance in the architecture of California's buildings at the coming Columbian Exposition."[20] These editorial comments initiated stylistic discussion for the upcoming California Building.

Deliberations began with "Old California Missions—I." Although unsigned, it was presumably written by one of the editors, possibly Willis Polk. The essay made special note of Mission Santa Barbara as "one of the best of the mission churches from an architectural point of view." Santa Barbara was one of the largest, most ambitious, and latest (1815-20) of the California missions. In a good state of preservation, it had also been observed by several of the editors during the late 1880s. Its severely classical design—with symmetrical, unadorned towers, clean surfaces, masonry construction and simple massing—appealed not only to Polk, but also to later Mission Revival architects.[21]

Architectural News also featured selected drawings, among which was "An Adobe Mission Church" by R. M. Turner.[22] (Fig. 27) The design, however, unlike those of Howard and Polk's earlier sketching group, did not employ Richardsonian Romanesque details. Oddly enough, the Presidio church at Monterey served as Turner's model. (Fig. 28) The sculptural portal, in particular, was common to the Southwestern missions, but was rarely found in California. By choosing a model more in keeping with academic principles of eighteenth-century Spain, Turner may have sought the same effect as had Leland Stanford. Again allusions were made to a "higher," more traditional style. Inscribed "Sketch Club of San Francisco. First Place," the drawing signified the interest of the club's participating architects.

At this time Charles Dudley Warner called for a reasoned approach to the question of style. In "The Winter of Our Content" for *Harper's,* he praised the adobes, simultaneously noting the inappropriateness of the wood-frame type. "Instead of adapting the houses and homes that the climate suggests, the new American comers have brought here from the East the smartness and prettiness of our modern nondescript architecture." Furthermore, by labeling the imported as "nondescript," he saw the attraction for architectural thinkers: a fresh direction for residential design. "The low house, with recesses and galleries, built round an inner court, or *patio,* which, however small, would fill the whole interior with sunshine and the scent of flowers, is the sort of dwelling that would suit the climate and the habit of life here." He analyzed the adobe ranch house in terms of its most distinctive components: the one-story height, the exterior arcades, and the interior patio. He implied a redesign of the American house. Warner's call for a California architecture was emphatic in a way unlike the suggestions of the 1880s.[23]

During 1891 *California Architect and Building News* ran a month-by-month mission series. An article on Sonoma, published in January, was the first discussion of its type to appear in the journal since 1884. Whereas the earlier essay had highlighted the picturesque, the 1891 article appraised the missions anew. Technical analysis accompanied section drawings, presenting a more accurate picture. In May the *News* assessed San Francisco's Mission Dolores. Again structural evaluation dominated the article. A shift in tone, however, had occurred with the reappearance of a romantic argument. During the following two months sentiment prevailed in evaluations of Missions San Carlos and San Antonio. (Fig. 29-31) Another shift occurred in August. Each of the next four articles focused on specific mission features—wall surfaces, arcades, and bell towers. A frantic search had begun for the "most architectural [details] of the old Spanish buildings in California." In December, the *News* gave it up as futile, commenting that there was in fact very little "architectural" about the California missions. Entitled "Mission Fragments," the essay reluctantly noted that the missions presented "no prodigality of design, no beauty of detail, but only the merest shadow of those towers and domes that lift the golden cross to kiss the summer sun in far off Spain." Together, the articles demonstrated well the range of misgiving and enthusiasm within the profession.[24]

The same year *American Architect and Building News* offered two similar series—"A Run Through Spain" and "Spanish Architecture." Concentrating not on the missions, but on Spanish architecture in general, author Charles A. Rich was especially entranced by the Spanish residential plan. "The planning of the

29-31 Mission San Antonio, sketch, section and plan published in *California Architect and Building News,* July 1891.

Founded by Father Serra as the third mission in the Franciscan network in 1771, San Antonio had witnessed intermittent periods of care and neglect. The mission had continued to prosper during the difficult years following Mexican independence, 1821-34. Yet it had fallen into ruin, 1835-48. Then during the next thirty years some repairs were undertaken—only to again be undone, 1882-1903. At the time of the study appearing in *California Architect and Building News* (1891), architects could still analyze the structural components of the mission and its planned layout, yet the dilapidated buildings also encouraged the more romantic, picturesque interpretation.

·MISSION·OF·SAN ANTONIO·

29

houses is peculiar, and in many ways charming, at least it is admirably adapted to the country and hot climate . . . as you enter and pass through a small hall you look directly into the *patio* or courtyard . . . often with an arched colonnade all around, and always full of plants and foliage, with the central fountain. Off from this court are the rooms in a variety of arrangement . . . the *patio* is susceptible of numerous treatments, and often in a most artistic manner." In subsequent articles Rich noted the patio as the most praiseworthy component of the plan. Commenting further, he assessed aesthetic qualities: "the beauties . . . of much of their plasterwork . . . [characterized by] . . . Absolute simplicity . . . [mark] . . . their design, and marvelous effects are obtained." Between April and June 1891 the journal continued to emphasize national interest in Spanish architecture through a presentation of historic monuments.[25]

Also in 1891 the California World's Fair Commission passed a resolution authorizing a separate state building at the Columbian Exposition in Chicago. *California's Monthly World's Fair Magazine* sanctioned a mission choice in May. "If the proposal to follow the style of architecture of the missions be adhered to a decidedly striking effect will unquestionably be produced."[26] On June 4 the San Francisco *Chronicle*, *Call* and *Examiner*, as well as the Los Angeles *Herald*, reported the results of a commission-sponsored competition. Only the *Chronicle* stated that the competition had been advertised, stipulating that "the design should be characteristic of the State." Two papers reported, "All the contestants evidently thought that to be typically Californian the building should have some of the old Mission features." At that point, however, choice of style was still unresolved. Indeed, it was not the major issue.

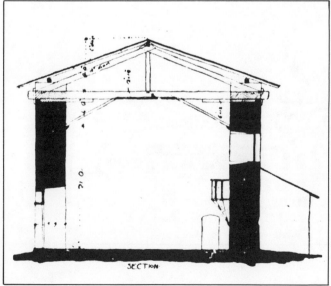

SECTION

30

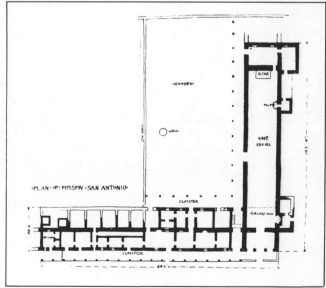

·PLAN·OF·MISSION·SAN ANTONIO·

31

Evidently California had yet to secure assurance from Chicago that it would actually be allowed a separate building. In addition, only nine plans had been submitted, demonstrating that the competition had not been well advertised after all. San Francisco architects, apparently the only ones really aware, had not responded enthusiastically to the idea of a state building.[27]

Five of the nine entries had attempted to incorporate mission imagery. Yet the responsible architects had obviously struggled. What features best represented the missions? The San Francisco newspapers agreed that Samuel Newsom's design had made the strongest impression among committee members. (Fig. 32) The *Examiner* noted, "Its particular charm is that it has an unmistakable Western look about it." Newsom's proposal was described as "a combination of the old mission type and that upon which the Salt Lake tabernacle was constructed. . . . The arcade is typical, having a roof of tiling." With elliptical plan, the building was to be a stuccoed wood-frame structure. An arcade extended around the exterior, while two fountains occupied each end of the auditorium. For the main entry Newsom borrowed the classical two-towered facade from Mission Santa Barbara. Two additional mission facades adorned the ends of the building. Unit massing, with paired towers and a central focus on the long axis, was nearly identical to the architect's previously published "Chateau en Espagne."[28]

Although the San Francisco newspapers of the time published terse descriptions of the remaining mission designs, no sketches have survived. Murray and Colby's proposal was for a two-story wood-frame building, stuccoed with tile roof. Exterior plasterwork was to simulate that of California's "old adobe buildings." Coupland Thomas planned a domed pavilion,

32 Samuel Newsom, entry for the first California Building competition, San Francisco *Examiner*, June 4, 1891. (California State Library, Sacramento)
One of the Northern California architects most captivated by the idea of a romantic (and eclectic) regional style, Samuel Newsom proposed a mission design for the California Building to be erected at the Columbian Exposition in Chicago in 1893. Towers and arcades dominated his Spanish vocabulary.

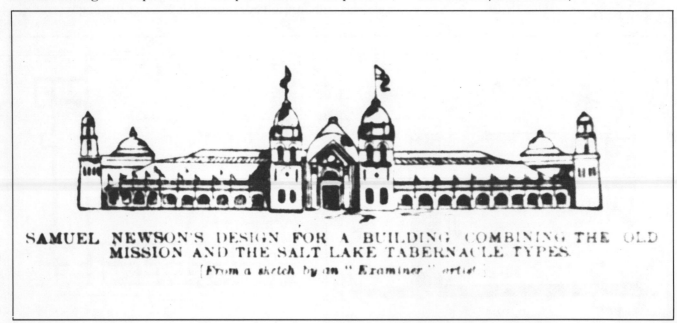

SAMUEL NEWSON'S DESIGN FOR A BUILDING COMBINING THE OLD MISSION AND THE SALT LAKE TABERNACLE TYPES
[From a sketch by an "Examiner" artist]

with a separate gallery designed "to represent an old mission church." W. K. Dobson struggled even more valiantly with the commission's stipulation that the proposals be characteristic of California. Designing a circular building capped with a large dome, Dobson added thirteen radiating wings representing the original Atlantic states. The whole composition symbolized the setting sun, while the main entrance was fashioned after the mission type. Dubbed the "Golden West," the design employed additional California symbols for the facade: "a bear of heroic size upholding a flagstaff, on the summit of which is perched a huge eagle with outspread wings." The final design, by W. C. Dickinson and Company, included tile roof and center tower, but construction was to be of brick with redwood.[29]

Of the remaining entries, the San Francisco *Chronicle* described that by P. A. Sioli as "similar to the plans . . . accepted for the Government building at Chicago;" while the *Examiner* described that by Ross and Gash as having "four arch ways constructed in the quaint Californian style." (Fig. 33) (Actually, Ross and Gash's entry was an adaptation of partner John Gash's 1881 tower for the Brush Electric Light Company in San Jose.) The *Call* noted that another design, that of E. W. Keeler, was to be "a cone-shaped building of very irregular form . . . surmounted by a tower." Decidedly the most bizarre of the attempts to stage a California exhibit was the ninth entry by B. McDougall and Son. "The entire structure is intended to represent in its shape a water-wheel such as was used for mining purposes in the early days of the State, as typical of that great industry. The not less important industry of fruit-growing is introduced by elevating the hub of the wheel in spherical form so as to bear a close resemblance to a huge orange. The buckets in the rim of the wheel will serve as booths for the different commodities of the State." The commission also accepted one late proposal, that of N. A. Comstock. His design incorporated a glass-covered interior court, archways supported by redwood columns, a brick and redwood-bark exterior, window sills of California onyx or marble, and a Spanish tile roof."[30]

Coverage of the proposals sent from San Francisco was scanty. On June 10 the *Chronicle* and the *Herald* reported, "The California State Commission laid before the ways and means committee today their plans for the State exhibit. They want to construct a building similar to the old missions." During the next several days, discussions continued. By June 12 the committee apparently had reached a decision. "The California Commissioners to-day had a conference with Supervising Architect Burnham and his consulting architects. The mission type of architecture seems to be favored as characteristic of the Pacific coast and distinctly Californian." Daniel H. Burnham, one of the most prominent architects in Chicago, was director of works and chairman of the consulting board for the fair. He

33 Ross and Gash, entry for the first California Building competition, San Francisco *Examiner*, June 4, 1891. (California State Library, Sacramento)

Ross and Gash's design for a California Building presented a somewhat unusual image. The first-story arcades were intended to resemble those of the Spanish adobe ranch house, while the four corner towers imitated an 1881 electric tower (designed by John Gash) in San Jose. The pavilion design showcased both past and present technologies, yet in so doing combined imagery that was utterly dissimilar. Scottish architect Thomas Patterson Ross had immigrated to San Francisco only the preceding year—the California Building proposal was among his first designs. It foreshadowed the architect's fascination with eclectic imagery—a fascination that would climax in his Chinatown designs of 1906-08.

and his firm, Burnham and Root, oversaw all architectural planning during 1890-93. The proposals of June 4 were sent on to Frederick Law Olmsted, landscape architect in charge of site choice, grounds layout and planting. On June 20 the Chicago *Tribune* reported that California had received the "largest amount of space excepting Illinois, because of its declared intentions." Reading between the lines, the case appeared closed—with Newsom's design the state choice. Yet by October, Californians were to read otherwise.[31]

Burnham's approval of the California proposals carried reservations. In 1892 the supervising architect would announce official guidelines for the individual state exhibits. Buildings were to be symmetrical, with rectangular plan unless the site called for an exceptional format. "The architecture should be dignified in style, formal rather than picturesque . . . The earlier styles that prevailed in this country such as the architecture of the old Spanish missions in Lower California and Mexico can with propriety furnish the motive for the buildings of the western and southwestern states." No California proposal had suggested appropriate materials while plans were more whimsical than accurate. Evidently Burnham was seeking a design that more closely followed the missions, one that did not have the inconsistencies present in the June entries. An article published in the San Francisco *Chronicle* in August 1891 further supports the argument that the Chicago architect was a demanding critic. Reporting progress on the Texas Building, the newspaper noted, "We shall adopt the style of one of our ancient Spanish missions . . . specifically that at San Antonio . . . In reproducing this famous landmark we can, by the use of staff [stucco], secure the exact effect of adobe, the material of

34-35 Ezra W. Keeler, suggestion for California Building, perspective and plan, *America Focalized*, 1891. (The Bancroft Library)

E. W. Keeler's proposal for a California Building was perhaps the most fantastic of all presented. An ornate Moorish Revival entrance accented a plain facade, while panoramic murals enlivened the interior. Only the small Engine and Electric Motor building, hidden at the pavilion's rear and out of the public's view, incorporated a mission architectural design: a mission tower set off this otherwise functional boiler house.

34

which it is built. Architect Burnham highly favors the plan."
Revision of the California proposals was all but a foregone
conclusion by the fall of 1891.[32]

The San Francisco *Call* and the Los Angeles *Herald* published an elaborately revised proposal during August and
October. Submitted by Ezra W. Keeler, it was both bizarre and
grandiose. Oversized Islamic gazebos—supported by redwood
columns and horseshoe arches—articulated the entry prome-
nade. (Fig. 34) A train was to carry visitors through the ser-
pentine arms of the exhibit, weaving in and out of man-made
mountains and a painted panorama of the missions. (Fig. 35)
Keeler's enthusiasm was boundless. To enhance the proposal's
attraction, the scheme was printed twice, once as *America
Focalized* and a second time as *California For Worldly Eyes in
1893*. Yet the plan was not satisfactory. M. H. DeYoung, one of
the fair's commissioners, wrote for *The Californian*: "Everywhere
the visitor wanders he should see California represented in
some shape . . . If this collective exhibit is placed . . . in an
attractive building whose architectural peculiarities will draw
attention . . . it . . . will finally and conclusively remove from
the Eastern and the foreign mind the damaging impression that
California is still a border region." Exterior design remained the
central issue. It had to say "California, " and Keeler's proposal
did not.[33]

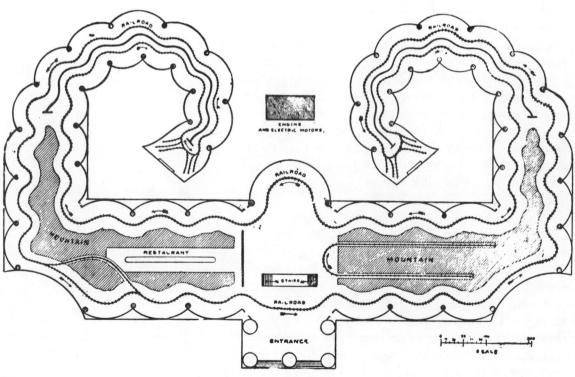

35

In early December 1891 the Los Angeles *Times* reported that the proposals had been set aside. "The question of style and plan of the building to be erected on California's site at the Fair were considered at length and all of the plans submitted by local architects last June were rejected and ordered returned to their makers, as none of them filled the requirements of the commission. A committee consisting of commissioners Phelan, Hatch, and Thompson was appointed to consult with leading architects and secure from them such ideas as to the building to be erected as would enable them to make some definite report at the meeting on the 10th." Meetings did in fact take place on the tenth, and again on the nineteenth. No firm conclusions were reached. During the month, too, architect W. J. Cuthbertson offered his solution. "It would be an almost exact reproduction of one of the Missions of California—the tower forming the entrance, the church the reception hall, cafe and wine sampling room and offices, while around the Patio would be grouped the one story exhibition galleries corresponding to the buildings around the garden of one of the California Missions." Even *The Wave*, a journal primarily of literary and political criticism, included a page of mission drawings in its December number.[34]

The California World's Fair Commission reconvened on January 12, 1892. Although "the building committee was not ready to present a definite report . . . Chairman Irving Scott asked an opinion of the board as to the most desirable style." The results proved interesting. "An informal vote being taken four out of the six members, namely, Irving Scott, R. McMurray, L. J. Rose, James D. Phelan, gave an unqualified verdict in favor of the Mission type, one commissioner voted for the 'progressive,' whatever that style may be, and Thomas H. Thompson voted in favor of the Romanesque. In order to bring the matter to a decisive issue Mr. Phelan moved that the commission should instruct architects that the California State building be of the old Mission type. An amendment was offered to substitute the word Moorish for Mission, but the amendment was lost. A second amendment substituting the words Moorish and Mission was carried, and it was decided to instruct architects to prepare plans of this unknown conglomerate style of architecture."[35]

The relative confusion of Mission, Moorish, and Romanesque had been a continuous theme throughout the 1880s. It had surfaced in the planning of Stanford University, as well as in other transitional designs. The final decision to adopt jointly the Moorish and Mission types—"this unknown conglomerate style"—for a second competition again revealed a willingness to compromise. The California missions alone did not satisfy those seeking a style with monumental scale and appeal, one which could be adapted to modern use and yet represent the historic landmarks of the state. Both the San Francisco

Examiner and *Call* published additional commentary on the results of the January 12 meeting. The *Examiner* noted, "The idea which the commission desires to convey by 'Mission and Moorish' is to have plans drawn as to ground work after the style of the missions and elaborated with trimmings of the ornate Moorish style." The *Call's* coverage differed only slightly: "The architects in planning their designs are to take from the Moorish school their ideas for ornamentation and from the Mission school their inspiration for working out something appropriate to and suggestive of California."[36]

On January 20, 1892, the California World's Fair Commission set forth formal instructions. Results appeared in the *Chronicle, Examiner,* and *Call* the next day, with the January issue of *California's Monthly World's Fair Magazine* outlining requirements. No mention was made of the preceding competition of May-June 1891. The commission's stipulations were respected by some, dismissed by others. The *Chronicle* reported, "So far as the Moorish and Mission style of architecture is concerned, most of the intending competitors said that it would make little difference what style was followed so long as a dome and an old Mission belfry are introduced, as the commissioners will not be any the wiser." A. Page Brown, Pissis and Moore, Samuel Newsom, and the Coxhead brothers expressed their intentions to submit designs.[37] (Fig. 36)

Evidently, the anonymous commentator for the *Chronicle* wrote with an accurate pen, even if with a caustic one. By February 12 the commission had announced that the proposal of A. Page Brown was the one preferred from among the thirty

36 Samuel Newsom, entry for the second California Building competition, January-February 1892. (Copy negative, collection of Richard Longstreth, Washington, D.C.; original, last in the collection of Elliot Evans, Oakland, 1974)

Samuel Newsom's January 1892 design proposal for a California Building is the only known extant for the second (and final) competition for the Columbian Exposition. Newsom adapted the facade of Missions San Antonio and Santa Barbara for the side entrances, and that of San Carlos de Borromeo for the main. Curiously, he simplified each mission facade almost diagrammatically, emphasizing outstanding features and giving all a two-towered symmetry. Newsom superimposed the mission facades on a large, elliptical pavilion with exterior and interior arcade.

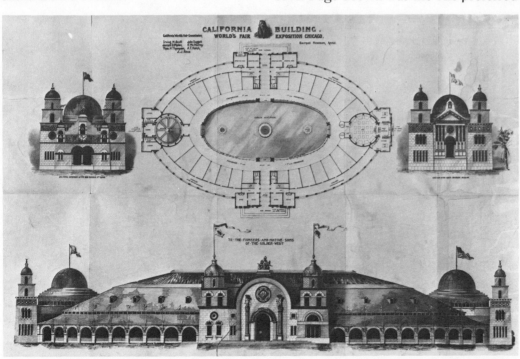

entries.[38] (Fig. 37-39) Second place went to B. McDougall and Son. (Fig. 40) Both Brown and the McDougalls relied upon an eclectic assemblage of mission elements to carry the California image. Brown's design featured an entrance on the long axis. Three mission facades, each differently towered, highlighted the scheme. Some design elements were taken from the missions, others borrowed from Richardsonian Romanesque. Most obviously, the architect drew upon Samuel Newsom's proposal of June 1891, rearranging the exterior components of the previous design. Shifting the Mission Santa Barbara facade from the main to the side entry, he embellished the long axis with a single tower and stepped gable. A quatrefoil window accented the design,[39] while solid mission piers replaced the colonetted characteristic of Richardson. Brown emphasized mission uniformity in the arcade, excluding the oversized, center entry common to the Richardsonian Romanesque.

Describing A. Page Brown's work, *California's Monthly World's Fair Magazine* declared that "The visitor will stand face to face with the California of yesterday . . .We will have a building whose architecture is all our own, which will take the beholder back to the days when the Fathers, with their old Missions, started the march of civilization in the Golden West." Each of the San Francisco newspapers praised the chosen design, illustrating Brown's Moorish-Mission California Building. *The*

37

CALIFORNIA STATE BVILDING
FOR THE WORLD'S COLVMBIAN EXHIBITION

38

37 A. Page Brown, 1893. Photograph published in *The Messenger*, April 1, 1893. (California Historical Society, San Francisco)

Educated at Cornell and a student draftsman for McKim, Mead and White, A. Page Brown first established an office in New York, from 1885 to 1889. He then traveled to San Francisco, where he maintained a successful practice until his early death in 1896. Several architects accompanied Brown from New York, including Willis Polk, Albert C. Schweinfurth, and Alexander F. Oakey. In addition, others passed through his office on the West Coast: Bernard Maybeck and Edward R. Swain were among the inner circle.

38 A. Page Brown, California Building, Columbian Exposition, Chicago, 1893. Perspective published in *American Architect and Building News*, July 30, 1892.

39 A. Page Brown, California Building. Elevation published in *American Architect and Building News*, December 15, 1894.

A. Page Brown's winning design for a California Building drew heavily upon the work of others. Exactly who contributed what remains unknown, but it is likely that Bernard Maybeck designed at least the dominant center dome. Maybeck had worked for Carrere and Hastings at the time of the Henry M. Flager Florida commissions, and the dome appears to be drawn from that of the Ponce de Leon Hotel. Maybeck also went to Chicago for Brown's office to supervise construction. Brown apparently drew the idea of superimposed mission facades for all entrances from Newsom, changing little and taking much. Perhaps only the strongly mission arcade, with linear core, was Brown's alone.

40 B. McDougall and Son, entry for the second California Building competition, February 1892. Perspective published in *American Architect and Building News*, September 3, 1892.

The McDougalls' entry demonstrated a heavier dependence on the established variety of the Queen Anne. Building mass was asymmetrically balanced, with design details recalling the Richardsonian Romanesque-Spanish Renaissance imagery of Stanford University and the Carrere and Hastings Florida resort hotels of the late 1880s. Simple arcades and *campanario*, taken more directly from the California missions, functioned as little-understood detail lost within the overall design.

39

40

41

Wave, however, published two anonymous editorials on February 13 that perhaps gave a more accurate picture of the award's reception among architects. The question of style, concerned with the creation of such a thing as Moorish-Mission, was still uppermost in discussion. One writer, dissatisfied with Brown's design, noted that other architects were disgruntled, that rumors of favoritism circulated. He bluntly stated that "the 'Mission' style is not recognized in architecture; the Mooresque has . . . a place, but it is neither a high nor an honorable one." The counteropinion characterized such bickering as unfortunate, quietly adding that "Mr. Brown's plans are as good, if not better, than any others submitted."[40]

Later in February, the Chicago *Tribune* noted that the California Building would be "characteristic of the great Pacific coast State, picturing in its exterior the California of the Padres and in its interior the California of today." Although no specific article indicated that Daniel Burnham had approved the proposal, it must be assumed that he had given his sanction by the middle of March. At this time a discussion related to the concluded competition appeared in *American Architect and Building News*. The writer did not sign the article, instead commenting only that he had entered the competition himself. His criticisms of the selected Moorish-Mission design were quite to the point. He granted that the commissioners' stipulation for a "building in the mission and Moorish style" was appropriate, that "however small the knowledge they had of that for which they were asking, they asked for the right thing." In analyzing the submitted designs, though, the architect felt that the commission had demonstrated weaknesses: "they allowed themselves to be carried away by a spread of canvas and a glare of color. Between the two extremes of a modern exhibition building and a combination of the several ruined mission buildings of California, there were all sorts of hybrids, and it was one of these . . . that the Commissioners considered most worthy." He continued, "I call it a hybrid because it is neither one thing nor the other; in mass, it has no resemblance whatsoever to a mission building. I say so with some confidence, having studied most of the mission buildings in California. The central part is more Japanese than anything else, and, as to the attaching a mission front to each extremity of the building, this only heightens the incongruity." Likening the design to a casino, the author concluded by observing that a Moorish-Mission style had not been achieved. In his evaluation, the California Building merely combined "frivolity and solemnity."[41]

Willis Polk is possibly the architect writing here. He, too, could well have composed the critical opinion presented earlier in *The Wave*. Having been involved in the late 1890 publication of *Architectural News*, and having also published his "Sketch of

An Imaginary Church of Southern California Type" in *Architecture and Building,* Polk had shown a serious concern with mission architecture and with the formulation of a mission style. Recognizing the probable future influence of the accepted design, he demonstrated succinctly the complexity inherent in the Northern California debates. After the erection of the California Building at Chicago—and even in the months between the design's acceptance and the fair—a "mission" model existed. For better or worse, the first phases of a transition towards a Mission Revival had been completed. California architects had inaugurated a "distinctive Mission style," a style derived from both the state's mission architecture and from the nationally known Richardsonian Romanesque.[42] Coincidentally, perhaps, the lean years within the profession also drew to a close in 1892, and with the resurgence in business came the willingness to offer clients the new imagery. In part, the imagery itself created the business.

Chapter Three

A Modern
Mission Style

*The jigsaw work of the Carpenteresque period
may be said to have seen its last days.*

Sumner P. Hunt, "Architecture," Los Angeles *Times*, January 1, 1897

RESIDENCE OF S. TAYLOR.
NEAR WINTERS CALIFORNIA

41

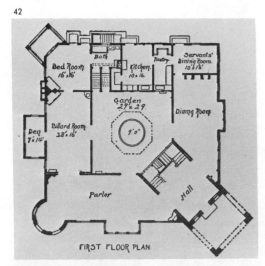

41-42 Percy and Hamilton, S. Taylor House, near Winters, 1892. Elevation and plan published in *California Architect and Building News*, September 1892.

An early Mission Revival design, the S. Taylor House incorporated a mixture of late Victorian and mission features. Circular tower, shuttered windows, and bays all drew upon the Queen Anne, while rectangular tower with porte-cochere emphasized the Spanish arch. Yet Percy and Hamilton's design was radically different in plan. Two stories of rooms enclosed an open garden with upper balcony.

F ollowing the competitions for the California Building, architects experimented more widely with Spanish design. A dependence on Richardsonian Romanesque faded as they worked toward a truly regional style. Yet prior to the close of the Columbian Exposition in December 1893, mission designs remained modest and few. Participating architects predictably were those involved in the late 1880s debates and in the 1891-92 competitions. This brief period, 1891-93, represented a second transitional phase, one which provided a direct springboard for the Mission Revival.

The San Francisco firm of Percy and Hamilton was among the first to adapt elements of Spanish architecture for residential design. Their "Residence of S. Taylor," published in *California Architect and Building News* in September 1892, broke away from past formulas with a two-story plan featuring an enclosed patio, fountain, and palm trees. (Fig. 41-42) Recognizing that a wood-frame structure could not successfully carry a Spanish design of this type, Percy and Hamilton employed concrete and stucco. The firm had acquired experience with reinforced concrete technology while working with Ernest Ransome on the Stanford Museum. Through their Stanford contract they were also necessarily familiar with the courtyard and arcades of the campus. (George Percy was furthermore an early advocate of concrete, publishing papers in the *Transactions of the Technical Society of the Pacific Coast* as early as 1888.) The *News* described the Taylor House as "designed in simple Spanish Style . . . the walls . . . coated with rough cement work on iron laths, giving it somewhat the appearance of an adobe house." In reality, it was only superficially Spanish. Built in Winters, the house incorporated the popular porte-cochere and San Francisco bay window.[1]

During 1893-94 other Northern California architects attempted a Spanish residential style. Polk and Polk drafted one of the earliest of the new designs—a San Francisco house for V. J. A. Rey. Fascinated by the missions since the 1880s, the father-and-son firm had contributed to design debate for the California Building. Indeed, the elder Polk (Willis Webb), as well as yet another relative (Daniel), had entered the 1892 competition. The Rey House made arches an integral part of the wall, clustering them at the corners to give a more striking effect to the remaining unadorned surface. A tile roof accented the building, while the open entryway and second-story veranda embodied the spirit of indoor-outdoor life associated with California.[2] (Fig. 43) Clarkson Swain followed the Polks' design with one of his own for "A Ranch House." (Fig. 44-46) Dated 1893 and published in *California Architect and Building News* in May 1894, his presentation included plans as well as perspective views. The patio was again the keynote, with a Spanish allusion enhanced by corner towers, balconies, mission gable, tile roof, and tropical foliage. Another "Spanish" design appeared in the July number of the *News*: T.E. O'Connor's "Study for a Chateau: Spanish Renaissance." O'Connor, too, challenged nineteenth-century traditions by showcasing an arcaded balcony and interior garden patio.

43 Polk and Polk, V. J. A. Rey House, San Francisco, 1894. Perspective published in *California Architect and Building News*, April 1894.

Polk and Polk's design for the V. J. A. Rey House employed only select Mission Revival elements: simple arches, planar walls, and tile roof. Perhaps just as emphatic were the Craftsman features: the wide overhanging eaves with exposed rafters, the columned pergola and the airy, projecting second-story balcony with simple stick balustrade. The residence foreshadowed not only the popularity of the Mission Revival, but also that of the Craftsman bungalow.

44-46 Clarkson Swain, "A Ranch House," 1893. Perspectives and plan published in *California Architect and Building News*, May 1894.

Clarkson Swain's design for a ranch house was one of the more elaborate that appeared in the early vogue of the Mission Revival. With a pastiche of detail, Swain created a fanciful hacienda, complete with vaquero. Yet, as had been true with the Taylor House near Winters, Swain's ranch house marked a radical departure in plan and elevation from the Victorian. Again two-story open courtyard with veranda along one side, arched windows facing the courtyard on both first and second stories, as well as entrance veranda and roof garden, all evoked the indoor-outdoor life style associated with the Mission Revival.

43

A RANCH HOUSE.

CLARKSON SWAIN - '93.

44

A CORNER IN THE COURT.

45

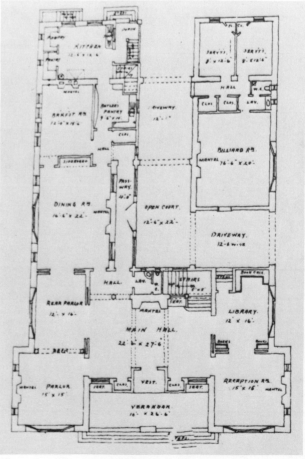

46

Residences with vague Spanish programs also surfaced in
Southern California. An 1894 Pasadena Board of Trade
pamphlet illustrated the Edwin Greble and Frank H. Valette
Houses erected during the preceding year. (Fig. 47-48) The
Greble residence included an arched veranda and corner tower,
while the Valette residence highlighted the horseshoe arch.
Both residences employed Spanish design elements in a
tentative fashion; however, they contributed to the imminent
vogue of the "Spanish Mission" style. *(American Architect and
Building News* later identified T. W. Parkes as the architect of
the Greble House.)[3]

By early 1892 Los Angeles architect C. L. Strange had also
applied a Spanish style to commercial design. Colonel G. G.
Green elaborately promoted his planned addition and renovation of Pasadena's Hotel Webster of 1887, renaming it the
Hotel Green. (Fig. 49) Commissioning architects Strange and
Carnicle, Green funded a Spanish extravaganza. C. L. Strange
was one of the few Southern California architects who had
entered the second competition for the California Building in
January-February 1892. Strange and Carnicle's Hotel Green
addition featured two towers, an entrance on the long axis and
both lower- and upper-story arcades. Massing resembled that of

47

47 T.W. Parkes, Edwin Greble House, Pasadena, 1893. Published in *American Architect and Building News*, February 11, 1899. [Demolished]

48 Frank H. Valette House, Pasadena, 1894. Published in Pasadena Board of Trade, *Pasadena and Environments*, 1894. (The Huntington Library) [Demolished]
    The Greble and Valette Houses of 1893-94 tentatively displayed the growing enthusiasm for a Spanish style. Arches and verandas were the primary design details associated with the new genre. In the Greble House, a multi-arched miniature mission *companario* functioned as the chimney.

49 Strange and Carnicle, Hotel Green, Pasadena, 1891-92, under renovation. Published in Pasadena Board of Trade, *Pasadena 1892, Crown of the Valley*, 1892. (Special Collections, University of California at Los Angeles) [Demolished 1935]
    In 1888 Edward Webster had backed construction of a promotional hotel in Pasadena near the Santa Fe depot—only to find himself short of the necessary funds. After borrowing money from G. G. Green in 1891, Webster still went bankrupt. Green, then owner of a partially finished two-story hotel, hired Strange and Carnicle and proceeded with renovation and enlargement.

the California Building designs submitted by Samuel Newsom in 1891 and A. Page Brown in 1892. The arcaded entrance, set off with a tower as its focal point, also recalled the recent proposals. The firm's use of Spanish motifs was recognized as transitional: "This being a semi-tropical climate, it necessarily combines the indolent and dreamy with the more severe in all that is undertaken. The Hotel Green shows plainly how powerfully this condition obtained in this favored section of the Western World. Here is a mingling of the old Spanish and Moorish type of architecture with the plainer and more substantial methods of the practical American." By 1894 the Hotel Green was variously described as a combination of the "Spanish and Moorish style" and as a blend of the "Spanish, Moorish and Mexican" types of architecture.[4]

In Northern California, just south of San Francisco, yet other designs represented a halfway point between the old and the new. (Fig. 50-51) Erected in early 1892 and early 1893, respectively, the granite arch and columbarium for the Cypress Lawn Cemetery in Colma were the work of B. McDougall and Son and Thomas Patterson Ross. In April 1892 the San Mateo County *Times-Gazette* described the arch as "close to the early Californian . . . the cupolas on the side and center columns being facsimiles of those on the old Mission churches." Again, the design was predictable. The family firm of Barnett McDougall had placed right behind A. Page Brown in the final awards in the California Building competition. As senior member of the partnership Ross and Gash, architect Ross had also partici-

50 B. McDougall and Son, Gateway to Cypress Lawn Cemetery, Colma, 1892. Published in *California Architect and Building News*, September 1896.

51 Thomas Patterson Ross, Columbarium, Cypress Lawn Cemetery, Colma, 1893. (J.W. Snyder: 1981)
McDougall and Son's granite arch highlighted the multi-acre Cypress Lawn Cemetery south of San Francisco. Other architectural components of the Olmstedian lawn-plan cemetery included Craftsman depot (for special funeral trains out of San Francisco) and Victorian Gothic church, with mission-style columbarium. T. Patterson Ross designed both church and columbarium. The entire complex survived the 1906 earthquake and still stands today. The gateway and columbarium are among the earliest mission-style structures extant anywhere.

52 Cotton Palace, Waco, Texas, 1894. Published in Fort Worth *Daily Gazette*, June 23, 1894. (Texas State Library, Austin)
The Waco Cotton Palace of 1894 drew conservatively, but heavily, upon the California Building erected for the Columbian Exposition in Chicago during the preceding year. Linear composition, towered mission entrance facades, and center dome were all taken directly. Yet arch proportions, second-story fenestration, end towers, and rectangular end cross-units derived from Richardsonian Romanesque, while the base for the center dome incorporated proportions and detailing taken from the Beaux-Arts.

pated in the competition of June 1891. One other Peninsula design, that of the Belmont School gymnasium of 1892-93, was also "mission." To date, its architect remains unknown.[5]

With the 1893 opening of the Columbian Exposition in Chicago, missionizing began in earnest. The fanfare and publicity that surrounded the California Building gave the Mission Revival the recognition it needed. James Phelan, vice-president of the California World's Fair Commission, described the state building as "a typical California building, and as marked in every feature as California itself." Rand, McNally and Company's handbook of the exposition, too, noted that the California Building was "a reproduction of the typical mission that was once common in that state," combining design units from Missions Santa Barbara, San Luis Rey, and San Luis Obispo. A mission style was no longer in the hands of just a few architects. Now architects throughout the country were exposed to the Franciscan imagery. The Cotton Palace, erected in Waco, Texas, in 1894, was only one tribute to the success of the California Building. (Fig. 52) Modeled directly after California's pavilion, it was designed to attract visitors to Texas. It proved an interesting statement. The 1893 Texas Building in Chicago was also a mission design. Based on a San Antonio mission, it should have provided the keynote for a Texas Mission Revival. Yet it was the California Building that captured the profession.[6]

Perhaps the final impetus for a Mission Revival came with the planning of the California Midwinter International Exposition. While in Chicago in 1893, M. H. DeYoung, commissioner for the Columbian Exposition and owner of the San Francisco *Chronicle*, had called a meeting of Californians,

51

52

proposing a similar fair for San Francisco in January 1894.[7] Promotion of the state's climatic and agricultural opportunities was intensified by an enthusiasm to demonstrate how quickly things happened in the West. Architects submitted eighteen sets of drawings in August 1893, with the resulting designs emphasizing Spanish, Moorish, and Mission motifs. Exoticism of this type was still associated with a mission style, so that one San Francisco *Call* reporter remarked that "Mission and Moorish" were "commonly included in the term 'Spanish.' "A design by Alexander F. Oakey, C. J. Colley and Emil S. Lemme was decidedly the most unusual. Discussed as "Moorish," the proposed building resembled a fanciful Mesopotamian ziggurat.[8]

Many of the same architects who had entered the second competition for the California Building also submitted designs for the Midwinter Fair. The commissions for the Manufacturers and Liberal Arts Building and the Administration Building were awarded to A. Page Brown. (Fig. 53-54) The first was to be Moorish with "four corner towers, richly and elaborately decorated," while the second was to be "Oriental in outline" with "Central Indian and Siamese" details. Having taken second place in the Chicago competition, B. McDougall and Son received the commission for the Fine Arts Building in

53 A. Page Brown, Manufacturers and Liberal Arts Building, Midwinter International Exposition, San Francisco, 1894. Perspective published in *California Architect and Building News*, September 1893.

54 A. Page Brown, Administration Building, Midwinter International Exposition. Perspective published in *California Architect and Building News*, September 1893.

Brown's Manufacturers and Liberal Arts Building repeated massing and general form from his California Building of the year before. Horseshoe arches and Richardsonian Romanesque grouped columns accented the structure. Yet the architect's eclecticism ranged wide—including castellated parapets and Beaux-Arts lantern capping the center dome. For his Administration Building, Brown drew upon Byzantine traditions, although whimsically adding his own details. Most bizarre was the winged griffin finial atop the building.

55 B. McDougall and Son, Fine Arts Building, Midwinter Internationl Exposition. Perspective published in *California Architect and Building News*, September 1893.

McDougall and Son's Egyptian-style Fine Arts Building was apparently the design of Charles C. McDougall alone. Charles, Barnett's eldest son, executed the principal work for the firm during these years. Battered tomb entrance dormers, pyramid roof, bundled reed columns resting on the backs of elephants, as well as corner gargoyles, were far removed from any Hispanic regional imagery, yet together these details contributed to the growing enthusiasm for all forms of exoticism.

an Egyptian style. (Fig. 55) Samuel Newsom designed the Agricultural and Horticultural Building (Fig. 56), deriving his ideas from "Mission building." Newsom had ranked fourth among the California Building entrants. Only Edward R. Swain, the architect for an "East Indian" and "Mission type" Mechanical Arts Building (Fig. 57), had not entered the earlier competition. He had, however, been employed by A. Page Brown at the time of the California Building commission.[9]

The *Overland Monthly* of November 1893 described the projected structures as "picturesque" and "of Oriental type." The two most significant were Brown's Manufacturers and Liberal Arts Building and Newsom's Agricultural and Horticultural Building. Predictably, Brown's design recycled his earlier work. A central dome accented the towered rectangular structure. In this instance, no distinctive mission features elaborated the design, although the architect did employ an arcade of Richardsonian Romanesque type. Sections of the roof were tiled, while horseshoe arch fenestration added to the effect. Newsom's pavilion proved more original. Like the missions, his building was to have an arcade of simple arches at ground level, with a similar arcade on the second story. A large elliptical dome set between four smaller ones accented the design. The only Richardsonian Romanesque element was a triple-arched entryway set upon colonetted piers. Brown's design was most often labeled "Moorish," while Newsom's design was either "Spanish Mission" or "Romanesque."[10]

Individual county buildings and minor exhibits at the Midwinter Fair more closely followed the mission model. Published examples included Taber's Photographic Gallery, buildings for Santa Barbara, Los Angeles, Southern California, Monterey, San Mateo County, and Alameda, as well as the Festival Hall,

54

55

56

57

56 Samuel Newsom, Agricultural and Horticultural Building, Midwinter International Exposition. Perspective published in *California Architect and Building News*, September 1893.

Retaining his preference for the elliptical plan, Samuel Newsom otherwise borrowed little from his designs for a California Building. Perhaps most characteristic of the architect were the eyelid eaves, a design motif often associated with Newsom residences.

57 Edward R. Swain, Mechanical Arts Building, Midwinter International Exposition. Perspective published in *California Architect and Building News*, September 1893.

Swain's Mechanical Arts pavilion also borrowed liberally from A. Page Brown's California Building. Here, however, Middle Eastern accents, including the pointed arch and the minaret, contradicted the otherwise strongly rectilinear composition.

58 Sumner P. Hunt, Southern California Building, Midwinter International Exposition. Perspective published in *Land of Sunshine*, July 1894.

Hunt's Southern California Building perhaps symbolized an intra-regional distinction felt by many. Not only did individual counties south of Monterey support the exposition, but together they sponsored a pavilion. Here an artist's rendering illustrates the building itself—with mission gables, arcades and tile roof—set in a sunny Southern California palm-studded landscape. Yet, the exposition was held in San Francisco's Golden Gate Park, from January to June. Thus the Southland's distinctive imagery would have been shrouded in heavy, damp fog much of the time. As the revival blossomed, however, Southern California did become its most appropriate stage.

58

the Moorish Mystic Maze and Boone's Wild Animal Arena.[11]
Even in instances where a mission design was not chosen for a
county exhibit, representative Moorish-mission entries often
highlighted submitted proposals. Perhaps the best articulated
of the mission type was the Southern California Building.
(Fig. 58) "The style of architecture of the building may be called
Spanish-American...and suggests Southern California by
reason of its resemblance to the best of our old missions."
Among the largest of the secondary exhibits, it featured plain,
massive arches, two mission gables, quatrefoil windows, a
center tower and tile roof. Sumner P. Hunt, the responsible
architect, would follow this design with others in the mature
Mission Revival and would become an active member of the
1890s Los Angeles preservation organization, the Landmarks
Club. *Land of Sunshine*, a Southern California popular journal
which began publication simultaneously with the final days of
the fair and carried numerous articles treating California architecture, described the Southern California Building as "one of
the leading attractions of the whole show."[12]

The Midwinter Fair of January-June 1894, held in San
Francisco's Golden Gate Park, was well publicized, with the
five major buildings illustrated and described in *American Architect and Building News, California Architect and Building News,*
and *Inland Architect and News Record.*[13] Regional coverage
was also extensive, including pamphlets, books, and numerous
articles. Editors recognized that a Californian style was in its
formative stages. By 1894 the Southern Pacific Company,
Land of Sunshine, and *Overland Monthly* popularized California
architecture, emphasizing its ties to climate, geography, and
Spanish tradition. Although it is little remembered, the San
Francisco Midwinter Fair was for California's architectural
development "not a warmed-over Columbian Exposition."[14] It
reinforced the tentative beginnings of a regional style.

Only Southern California's involvement was needed to
complete the transitional process. In 1894 the Merchants'
Association of Los Angeles hosted a "Fiesta" to enliven the
depressed economy. Unabashedly a promotional attempt to
attract visitors from San Francisco's Midwinter Fair, the celebration found itself in the capable hands of Charles Fletcher
Lummis. Whereas the fair had employed mission imagery in its
pavilions, the fiesta relegated the theme to parade floats. An
official program described Calfiornia's past as beginning with
"the dreamy halcyon days of the missions, the drowsy pueblos
and the peaceful quiet life of the Ranchos." A brief history of
the missions followed, with "The Old Mission" float illustrated
in the text. The *campanario* (bell wall) from San Gabriel highlighted its detail. A success, the 1894 fiesta fostered a second
celebration the next year. Lummis, by this time editor of *Land*

of Sunshine, planned an elaborate "Pageant of the Pacific."
Sumner P. Hunt, architect of the Southern California Building
at the Midwinter Fair, collaborated, helping to arrange nineteen
floats representing the West Coast. The missions occupied a
prime spot in the parade, again with an individual float modeled
after Mission San Gabriel. (Fig. 59) The overall thematic treatment was architectural, including Inca, Aztec, Mexican, Zuni,
Pueblo, Mission, and Spanish displays. After 1895 many
Southern California cities held annual fiestas, thereby
increasing the public's familiarity with mission architecture.[15]

The Columbian Exposition, the Midwinter Fair, and the Los
Angeles fiestas established a precedent for state-sponsored
buildings. In the successive expositions held at Buffalo (1901),
St. Louis (1904), Portland (1905), and Seattle (1909), California's pavilion was Mission Revival. (Fig. 60) In each case a
different interpretation of mission architecture was set forth. In
1911 *Architect and Engineer* even published a sketch for a
mission-style California Building in London.[16] (Fig. 61)
Lessons learned through these temporary structures both
initiated and enhanced the early years of the Mission Revival.

Immediately following the Chicago and San Francisco fairs of
1893 and 1894, Northern California architects explored a
mission style through a range of eclectic designs. Residential
commissions, 1895-99, were particularly conservative. Perhaps
architects remained too close to the debates of the late 1880s
and early 1890s to step outside the professional confusion of
Spanish, Moorish, and Mission. In any case, architectural
journals published only a small group of Spanish-Mission
houses. These included Albert C. Schweinfurth's Hacienda del
Oso of 1896, Samuel Newsom's J. M. Lane and Parker Houses

59 Sumner P. Hunt, ''Missions of California,'' parade
float, Fiesta de Los Angeles, 1895. Perspective published in *La Fiesta de Los Angeles,* April 1895. (Special
Collections, University of California at Los Angeles)

Just as Hunt had represented Southern California
through his Midwinter International Exposition pavilion,
he was in the design forefront with his architectonic
parade floats for the Los Angeles fiestas. Hunt worked
with Charles Fletcher Lummis to create the extravaganza, this time set in mission heartland.

60 Samuel and J. Cather Newsom, California Building,
Louisiana Purchase Exposition, St. Louis, 1904. Perspec-
tive published in San Francisco Architectural Club,
Catalogue of the Second Annual Exhibition, 1903. (Col-
lege of Environmental Design Library, University of
California, Berkeley)

The Newsoms again adapted the regional favorite
for their St. Louis pavilion. Taking the two-towered
facade of Mission Santa Barbara quite literally, the
architects added less formidable ''hacienda'' wings to
either side.

61 Charles E. Hodges, ''California Building, London,
England,'' *Architect and Engineer,* July 1911.

Charles E. Hodges had worked as a draftsman for
Shepley, Rutan and Coolidge during the tenure of the
Stanford commission. Later, during the 1893-1907
years, Jane Stanford hired Hodges as resident campus
architect. Although the specific purpose of the London
California Building remains unknown, its appearance is
not a complete surprise. Hodges himself was born and
educated in England and during 1908-09 traveled
abroad.

59

CALIFORNIA BUILDING, LOUISIANA PURCHASE EXPOSITION
Newsom & Newsom, Architects

60

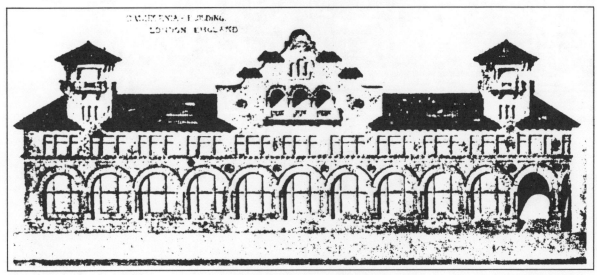

61

of 1897, J. Murray's "Country Residence" of 1898 and Havens and Toepke's untitled design of 1898.[17] (Fig. 62-64)

In Southern California the 1895-99 years took on a much different cast. It was here that the Mission Revival blossomed—especially in its application to residential design. T. W. Parkes, designer of the Greble House in 1892-93, executed another commission in a mission style in 1895 for Mrs. Meeker of Pasadena.[18] Reminiscent of the earlier design, the Meeker House included a similar arcade and tile roof. Parkes extended the arcade across the entire facade, giving the design unity. The individual arches, too, were simple, more closely recalling those of the missions. Another house—for W. S. Tevis in Bakersfield, by architect Henry A. Schulze—also used lower-story arcades, an upper-story quatrefoil window, and tile roof. (Fig. 65) Published in *California Architect and Building News* in April 1895, the design evoked the missions without imitating them. Schulze designd arch and pier as a single unit, thus creating a unified, planar effect complementary to the

62 Samuel Newsom, "Residence for J. M. Lane," *California Architect and Building News*, May 1897.
The 1897 Newsom design epitomized the late nine-teenth-century Spanish image. A proposed residence for J. M. Lane (possibly never built, location unknown) included large formal courtyard, front veranda, squat Queen Anne corner tower, rear mission gables and arbor.

63 J. Murray, "Country Residence," *California Architect and Building News*, November 1898.

64 Havens and Toepke, untitled design, *California Architect and Building News*, November 1898.
Two San Francisco firms, J. Murray and Havens and Toepke, presented Mission Revival designs for *California Architect and Building News* in late 1898. Both clung tenaciously to well-accepted building forms, applying a Spanish veneer through gables, quatrefoils, towers, and tile.

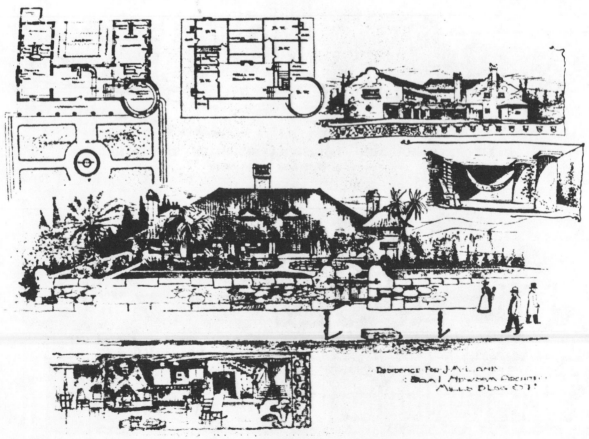

RESIDENCE FOR J. M. LANE
SAM'L NEWSOM ARCHITECT
MILLS BLDG S.F.

62

J. Murray, Archt S.F.

63

64

65

rectilinear form. Upper-story balconies added to the open atmosphere, while the quatrefoil window served as the one decorative accent.

Frederick L. Roehrig also designed a mission-style house in 1895; however, his interpretation was distinctly different from that of Parkes or Schulze.[19] (Fig. 66) The W. C. Stuart House in Pasadena was much more flamboyant and curvilinear, depending upon a sculptural use of stucco on metal lath. Mission gables and round-arched windows in oval frames maximized this effect. Both the severe and sculptural approaches, as illustrated through the work of Parkes, Schulze,

65 Henry A. Schulze, ''Los Portales,'' W. S. Tevis House, Bakersfield, 1895. Perspective published in *California Architect and Building News*, April 1895. [Demolished]

One of the more ambitiously designed early Mission Revival houses, the residence of W. S. Tevis, a wealthy San Francisco real estate man, was everything the Valette House was not. Henry A. Schulze relied heavily upon the arcade. Indeed, ''Los Portales'' meant ''the arcades.'' Schulze practiced in San Francisco, and was best known for his work with reinforced concrete and issues of proper building inspection.

66 Frederick L. Roehrig, W. C. Stuart House, South Orange Grove Avenue, Pasadena, 1895. Published in *House and Garden*, September 1907. [Demolished]

Roehrig's W. C. Stuart House marked a Pasadena departure from the spare design work of T. W. Parkes. The Stuart House, like others on South Orange Grove Avenue, was published many times in wide-ranging journals, as well as in local board of trade pamphlets. It must have come to represent the revival in many minds.

67 Mausard-Collier, ''La Mita,'' John W. Mitchell House, Cahuenga, 1896. Published in *Land of Sunshine*, May 1896. (California State Library, Sacramento) [Demolished]

The house of Virginia lawyer John W. Mitchell may well have been one of the very few residences built in the short-lived boom town of Cahuenga. Mapped and partially laid out in 1887-88, Cahuenga featured circular and semi-circular drives with plans for ambitious residential neighborhoods. Coincidentally, Mitchell arrived at this same time, 1887. *Land of Sunshine* published the Mitchell House as ''La Mita,'' a name that was likely the corruption of ''El Mito''—the myth. The name was indeed apt, for in only a few years the Cahuenga Land and Water Company went bust, and the almost non-existent town faded into obscurity. Ironically, however, it was Hollywood—the maker of modern legend—that would occupy the site by the early twentieth century.

66

and Roehrig in 1895, continued as related, but aesthetically dissimilar, interpretations of the Mission Revival.

In 1896 several other residences appeared in the Los Angeles area. *Land of Sunshine* published "La Mita" that year, citing the engineer as Mausard-Collier. (Fig. 67) The Cahuenga mansion, featuring towers and mission gables, was wrapped in arcades. Another residence of the same year continued this approach to a mission design. The Gail Borden House in Alhambra retained bay windows while employing gable and tower details. (Fig. 68-69) As a finishing touch, L.B. Valk and Son applied molded stucco ornament over all. A more austere design of 1896 was the Hosmer House in Pasadena, by Charles and Henry Greene, which combined mission gables with classical columns and curved pediments, a design perhaps inspired by the facade of Mission Santa Barbara. In 1897 the Greene brothers designed another house for Frances Swann. It, too, demonstrated a fascination with Mediterranean styles.

67

68

69

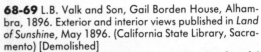

68-69 L.B. Valk and Son, Gail Borden House, Alhambra, 1896. Exterior and interior views published in *Land of Sunshine*, May 1896. (California State Library, Sacramento) [Demolished]

Built for New Yorker Gail Borden, the fanciful Spanish-style residence captured the romantic enthusiasm pervading Southern California. Borden, grandson of the Gail Borden of condensed milk fame, had moved to California in 1895, settling in the young Los Angeles suburb of Alhambra. By 1897 Borden had established himself as a mining capitalist.

Although Greene and Greene became known for their Craftsman bungalows, Charles Greene continued to admire mission design into the first decade of the twentieth century.[20]

The Mission Revival took hold in Southern Calfornia in 1897. In that year the Midwinter Number of the Los Angeles *Times*, January 1, included a thorough discussion of the past year's building. Eliza A. Otis, wife of *Times* owner Harrison Gray Otis, wrote, "Among these first class residences an old-new type is rapidly growing in favor. It is the modernized adobe, of the old Spanish style of architecture, with the beautiful patio, or court in the center. They are two stories in height, with towers and turrets, broad windows and wide verandas . . . The rooms all open upon the lovely patio." A

62

70 Sumner P. Hunt, undated. (Security Pacific National Bank Photograph Collection, Los Angeles Public Library)

Born in New York, Sumner P. Hunt traveled to Los Angeles in 1889 and there worked for Caukin and Haas (as had John Galen Howard in 1887-88). During the 1895-1900 years he designed in partnership with Theodore Eisen and A. W. Eager, and after the turn of the century with Eisen alone. Sumner P. Hunt authored numerous theoretical articles on the early mission style, assuming a role in Southern California parallel with that of Willis Polk in the North.

71 Locke and Munsell, D. M. Smyth House, Pasadena, 1897. Published in *American Architect and Building News*, February 4, 1899. [Demolished]

The D. M. Smyth House incorporated several Mission Revival features, including prominent quatrefoil and first-floor verandas. Yet the circular corner tower, as well as the general massing of the building, betrayed the established forms of McKim, Mead and White's residential Shingle Style.

decade earlier Mrs. Otis had also written for the *Times*, praising Mission Santa Barbara and its "esteemed air of antiquity."[21] There was more to come.

Sumner P. Hunt also reviewed emerging architectural trends in the 1897 Midwinter Number. Hunt assumed the articulate role in Los Angeles that Willis Polk had assumed six years earlier in San Francisco. (Fig. 70) He noted, "The jig saw work of the Carpenteresque period may be said to have seen its last days." Continuing, the architect compared Los Angeles with other growing cities, finding one exception, "the decided and encouraging tendency to develop a local style from the adaptation to our requirements of the Renaissance of Southern Europe. This is directly resultant from the presence throughout Southern California of the mission buildings put up one hundred years ago by the Spanish fathers of the Catholic church." Hunt further deliberated the aesthetics of stucco and concrete. He cited the missions as "an ever-present illustration of the beauty of a form and material radically different from the result to be obtained from the wooden constructions so commonly used in American suburban work." Analyzing "cement-plaster" and its application to metal lath, Hunt asserted that stucco could simulate "Spanish," "Mooresque," or "Italian Renaissance" styles, which he defended as most appropriate to the climate and geography of Southern California.[22] Accompanying the Otis and Hunt articles, the *Times* also published a Pasadena residence, the D. M. Smyth House by Locke and Munsell.[23] (Fig. 71) The Smyth residence was the first mission-style house to be illustrated by the *Times*. In the same year the firm of Blick and Moore executed a Mission Revival residence for Frank Emery of Pasadena. The Emery House was republished throughout the vogue of the Mission Revival.[24]

70

71

As 1898 began, the Los Angeles *Times* once again directed its attention to the question of suburban design raised in its pages by Sumner P. Hunt the preceding year. In the January 1 issue of the new year, architect John Kremple traced the state's architectural history from the adobes through the imported East Coast styles to the recent mission types, emphasizing California's temperate climate and the attendant need to design suitable residences. He remarked that even after the railroad had allowed Southern California to establish an independent economic base, "still Americans would not be Romans in Rome, but insisted on building Queen Anne houses . . . They could not believe that ours was a country where nature intended them to live in the open air, and that an abundance of porch room, a patio or inclosed court, rooms with large window openings, etc., were some of the requisites of a comfortable home in Los Angeles or Southern California." Like Hunt, Kremple cited a relationship between the mission model and stucco and concrete. An illustration of one of the architect's recent commissions accompanied the article. Described as "designed after the style affected by the adobe and mission builders," it proved to be the Otis House on Wilshire Boulevard in Los Angeles.[25] (Fig. 72) The Otis family's choice of style reflected their enduring enthusiasm. A somewhat whimsical design, the residence resembled the mission work of Frederick L. Roehrig.

In 1898, also, the Pasadena Board of Trade published another Mission Revival residence on Orange Grove Avenue— Blick and Moore's H. B. Sherman House. (Fig. 73) Here, as in the Otis House by John Kremple, Blick and Moore emphasized curvilinear mission details. However, unlike Kremple, this firm simplified gable and arcade, relying upon a crisp geometry as they had during the previous year. In 1899 *American Architect and Building News* featured the Sherman House as another example of the style.[26]

Pasadena and Los Angeles were not the only sites of late 1890s Mission Revival residential design. Somewhat of an anomaly was a row of five houses in Santa Barbara designed by A. Page Brown. (Fig. 74) Commissioned by W. H. Crocker of San Francisco as vacation houses, these residences apparently constituted a singular instance of Mission Revival in Santa Barbara of 1894-98. Brown combined sculptured ornament with a rather severe rectilinear treatment, emphasizing mission details in the two structures that bracketed the group. Banked windows, unadorned wall surface above the verandas, chimneys, and jutting roof lines all created a restless interaction between the vertical and horizontal lines of the buildings. These Mission Revival houses were like no others executed at this time.[27]

72

73

72 John Kremple, Harrison Gray Otis House, Los Angeles, 1898. Published in *Craftsman*, February 1904.

Like many others, German architect John Kremple arrived in Southern California during the boom, 1886-87. His residence for newspaper magnate Harrison Gray Otis displayed a flamboyantly sculptural approach to the Mission Revival. In addition, the house illustrated Kremple's commitment to an appropriately regional residence type, as well as to the innovative building technology of stucco and concrete. In the following decade the architect designed the second *Times* building in Los Angeles for Otis.

73 Blick and Moore, H. B. Sherman House, Pasadena, 1898. Published in *American Architect and Building News*, International Edition, February 18, 1899. (Avery Architectural Library) [Demolished]

J. J. Blick and Lester S. Moore collaborated in their design of the H. B. Sherman House. Yet another Mission Revival residence for Pasadena, the large two-story structure blended the Craftsman with the mission. Gabled dormer, like the attached veranda, still stood out as grafted. Yet even with its flaws, the Sherman House was one of a very few California Mission Revival residences (each from Pasadena) chosen for illustration in the International Edition of *American Architect and Building News*.

74 A. Page Brown, W. H. Crocker Houses, Santa Barbara, 1894-98. Published in *American Architect and Building News*, Imperial Edition, January 15, 1898.

Brown's five Mission Revival Santa Barbara vacation houses were among the last designs executed by his firm before the architect's early death. San Francisco banker William Henry Crocker commissioned the mission-style residential block literally in full view of Mission Santa Barbara, a fact revealed by contemporary published photographs of the houses.

74

American Architect and Building News illustrated two of the Crocker residences in the advertisement pages of its Imperial Edition in 1898. One of these is nearly identical to the Jas. H. Adams House published in the Pasadena Board of Trade booklet of 1897. (Fig. 75) Differing only slightly in the proportions of several details, the Santa Barbara and Pasadena houses may have been executed simultaneously, possibly by the same architect. It certainly appears as if the houses, one hundred miles apart, were carried out by one or more designers working from a single set of plans. The architect for the Adams residence, sold by 1901 and known in subsequent literature as the Harrison T. Kendall House, has remained anonymous.[28]

By 1899 Mission Revival was quickly becoming accepted. It received extensive coverage in the January 1 Midwinter Number of the *Times*. "The advances made in architecture in the United States in the past twenty-five years are amazing, and nowhere has that advance been more marked than in Southern California, where a distinctive style has been evolved by methods that stand the test of artistic sincerity." In February, *American Architect and Building News* published Mission Revival houses nationally and internationally. Both the Greble House of 1893 by T.W. Parkes and the Smyth House of 1897 by Locke and Munsell were included in the journal, as was another residence, the D.R. Cameron House in Altadena by Frederick L. Roehrig. However, it was the architecture of Blick and Moore that received the most thorough coverage, with several of their 1897-99 Mission Revival houses illustrated. The year 1899 was a watershed for the development of Mission Revival suburban design. Although the style was to become immensely popular, *American Architect and Building News* never again acknowledged it as avant-garde.[29]

Although residential design became the most widespread type in the following years of the Mission Revival, architects also adapted the style for railroad stations, hotels, schools, and business buildings. After publicity of the California Building, both the Atchison, Topeka and Santa Fe and the Southern Pacific commissioned Mission Revival stations. In 1893 J. B. Mathison and George H. Howard designed the Burlingame depot for the Southern Pacific, while B. F. Levet designed the San Juan Capistrano station for the Santa Fe. (Fig. 76-77) Mathison had entered the California Building competition of 1892 and thus had previous experience with mission design. Levet, however, was strictly a company architect. Both buildings were completed and published in 1894. Employing similar arcades, tile roofs, towers, and gables, each railroad played to an audience of tourists and immigrants. The railroads erected numerous Mission Revival stations during the first and second decades of the twentieth century.[30]

75

76

75 James H. Adams House, South Orange Grove Avenue, Pasadena, c.1894-97. Published in *Pasadena Board of Trade, Illustrated Souvenir Book*, Los Angeles, 1898 . (California State Library, Sacramento) [Demolished]

The Adams House remains a mystery. Who designed it? Perhaps an architect from the San Francisco office of A. Page Brown? Or perhaps an admiring imitator? Curiously, the residence is nearly identical to the southernmost house in the Crocker block located one hundred miles away in Santa Barbara.

76 Mathison and Howard, Southern Pacific depot, Burlingame, 1893-94. Perspective published in *California Architect and Building News*, April 1894.

77 B. F. Levet, Atchison, Topeka and Santa Fe depot, San Juan Capistrano, 1893. Perspective published in the Los Angeles *Times*, October 28, 1894.

Designed for the Southern Pacific and for the Santa Fe, Mathison and Howard's and B. F. Levet's mission-style depots of 1893-94 were the first to introduce the revival to the railroads. Interestingly enough, even with the highly competitive rate wars and promotions, adoption of the Spanish imagery was simultaneous. No doubt the popularity of A. Page Brown's California Building in Chicago during 1893 stimulated the design of the many stations that soon followed.

The new railway station.

77

After the transitional attempt at a Moorish-Spanish style in the 1892 addition to the Hotel Green in Pasadena, architects also applied the Mission Revival to hotel design. W. D. Van Siclen presented his design for "A Country Hotel" (Fig. 78) in *California Architect and Building News* of March 1895. The design, never executed, incorporated towers, gable, tile roof, arched and quaterfoil windows as well as arcades. Samuel Newsom designed a "Proposed Hotel near Golden Gate Park" reminiscent of his previous exposition work in the mission style. Published in May 1895, the design foreshadowed the lavishness of plan and detail that Arthur B. Benton would expend upon the Mission Inn of Riverside in 1901. In Southern California Eisen and Hunt proposed the "Adams Street Tourist Hotel" (Fig. 79), employing all the mission details once again. The hotel was featured in R. B. Dickinson's *Los Angeles of Today Architecturally* of 1896, as was the Hollenbeck Home for the Aged by Morgan and Walls.[31] (Fig. 80)

Perhaps the most influential hotel design of these years was yet another addition to the Pasadena Hotel Green. In 1898 Frederick L. Roehrig designed a mission-style annex for the older hotel and its 1892 Spanish-Moorish addition. (Fig. 81-82) Described like the addition that preceded it as "Moorish . . . from top to bottom," Roehrig's design elaborated upon C. L. Strange's ideas by including sixty wrought-iron balconies, intricate stucco ornament, a roof garden and copper domes atop the southern towers. Two more additions were planned for the Hotel Green, one partially completed and one only projected. A 1903 Pasadena Board of Trade souvenir book illustrated the planned complex in a lavish color lithograph.[32]

78 W. D. Van Siclen, ''A Country Hotel,'' *California Architect and Building News, March 1895.*

The proposed hotel of 1895 illustrated a trend that would soon take hold in Southern California: the erection of large-scale Mission Revival tourist hostelries. Van Siclen's design featured an array of the standard Spanish elements, including towers, tile roof, gables, arcades, and quatrefoils. Yet, for Northern California, the Mission Revival hotel on such a grand scale was not to be.

79 Eisen and Hunt, ''Adams Street Tourist Hotel (Proposed),'' in R. B. Dickinson, *Los Angeles of Today Architecturally*, 1896. (Special Collections, University of California at Los Angeles)

80 Morgan and Walls, Hollenbeck Home for the Aged, Los Angeles, 1896. Perspective published in R. B. Dickinson, *Los Angeles of Today Architecturally*, 1896. (Special Collections, University of California at Los Angeles)

In Southern California, however, the tourist hotel, as well as more permanent housing for the elderly, was immediately well received. Many Easterners wintered in Los Angeles, Pasadena, Santa Barbara, and surrounding towns. In addition, others came for their health, for the climate, for easier retirement. Eisen and Hunt's design captured the grandeur of the hotels not yet built, while Morgan and Walls's home epitomized the phenomenon itself.

81-82 Frederick L. Roehrig, Hotel Green annex, Pasadena, 1898. (K. J. Weitze: 1976)

Frederick L. Roehrig's design for an elaborate addition to the Hotel Green represented not only the tourist hotel boom, but also the closely allied promotional efforts of the railroads. As early as 1891, the Atchison, Topeka and Santa Fe had named its Chicago (via Kansas City) to Los Angeles train the California Special. By 1893 it had become the California Limited. And under the 1898 Moorish porte-cochere of the Hotel Green, the Limited made a formal stop, delivering its eager passengers to their very door.

79

80

81

82

California schools also began to adopt the Mission Revival. At the 1893 Columbian Exposition, California had included a display of school architecture as a part of its exhibit. Entitled "Casa de Rosas" it evidently inspired the planning of the Froebel Institute in Los Angeles of 1894. Designed by Sumner P. Hunt, the institute (Fig. 83) was likely the first mission-style school in the state—one which stylistically, structurally, and philosophically foreshadowed the scores that followed. Stucco on metal lath, the school included a patio, round-arch windows, and arcades. Coincident with adoption of mission design, there was also an underlying idealism: the indoor-outdoor setting would encourage learning. "Casa de Rosas was pronounced by the judges at the Columbian Exposition a model of school architecture . . . it is also a perfect bit of Moorish architecture . . . Children in the atmosphere of its beauty alone can not fail to be uplifted." By September 1895 *Land of Sunshine* presented the institute as typifying the direction that California schools should take in the future.[33] In 1897 the same journal published "Los Baños," which it featured as representative of San Diego's schools of "modern architecture." Actually, Los Baños had only the slightest of educational affiliations. For San Diegans it was better known as the city bath house.[34] (Fig. 84)

The following year George Costerisan designed a Mission Revival high school for Long Beach. (Fig. 85) Like the 1896 Mitchell House "La Mita," Long Beach High School illustrated an abuse of concrete technology through a haphazard application of mission details. Nonetheless, educators saw the school as a progressive addition to the community. In an article on education in Southern California, the president of the Los Angeles Board of Education commented, "Long Beach has a new high school in the Mission style of architecture, in which not only that city but this whole region rejoices." By 1897-99, libraries, too, were designed in the Mission Revival. A prominent example was the A. K. Smiley Public Library in Redlands.[35] (Fig. 86)

83

83 Sumner P. Hunt, Froebel Institute, Los Angeles, 1894. Published in *Land of Sunshine*, September 1895. [Demolished]

As had been true for the earliest Mission Revival residences, Hunt's institute explored a mission style tentatively. In exterior appearance the school offered only a series of arches to tie it to the Spanish architectural trend. Yet on the inside an open courtyard again emphasized the significant changes made to the plan. Named "Casa de Rosas"—"House of Roses"—the Los Angeles Froebel Institute capitalized on the imagery of Southern California.

84

85

84 Hebbard and Gill, ''Los Baños,'' San Diego, 1897. Published in S. T. Black, *San Diego County California*, Chicago, 1913, Volume 1. (California State Library, Sacramento) [Demolished]

Designed by Hebbard and Gill in 1897, the bath house known as Los Baños in San Diego provided civic entertainment and medicinal relief. The inside tank was tile-lined and featured copper-plated toboggans for the guests. Cold water from the bay was pumped through the adjacent streetcar powerhouse to cool condensers, then cycled hot into the bath house. In 1898 Swedish gymnast and masseur W. Ankarstrand opened an institute at Los Baños offering scientific massage, electric and medicated baths, fomentations, and salt glows. The fanciful Mission Revival design was one of Irving Gill's first in California.

85 George Costerisan, Long Beach High School, Long Beach, 1898. (Security Pacific National Bank Photograph Collection, Los Angeles Public Library) [Demolished]

Full-fledged Mission Revival schools did not take long to make an appearance. By 1898 Los Angeles architect George Costerisan had designed a high school for Long Beach replete with all the stylistic keynotes of the revival.

86 T. W. Griffith, A. K. Smiley Library, Redlands, 1897-99. (K. J. Weitze: 1978)

Just prior to the turn of the century, educator and philanthropist Albert Keith Smiley donated the needed funds for a city library in Redlands. Like many early Mission Revival showpieces, the library dominated a sparsely built-up skyline—a skyline filled mostly with groves of orange trees.

86

Other types of Mission Revival public buildings also made their appearance following the opening of the Columbian Exposition. In 1893 A. Page Brown designed the St. Claire Club in San Jose, while in 1894 Fresno sponsored a civic water tower with Spanish detail. The tower was most unusual. Designed by Chicago architect George W. Maher, the hundred-foot-high brick structure alluded to Spanish architecture through its tile roof and multi-arch decorative cornice. Maher may well have added these details to make his design "Californian." Certainly, he would have been familiar with the new mission style after observing the California Building at the Columbian Exposition. (Fig. 87) In November 1895 *California Architect and Building News* published B. J. S. Cahill's design for a fraternal meeting hall in San Francisco. (Fig. 88) Mission in style, it showcased the two-towered facade that would become a commonplace accent in the early twentieth-century streetscape. In 1896 Edward R. Swain, designer of the Mechanical Arts pavilion at the Midwinter Fair, contributed his Moorish-Mission Golden Gate Park Lodge. Percy and Hamilton

87 George W. Maher, water tower, Fresno, 1894. (K. J. Weitze: 1980)

Fresno's water tower of 1894 was indeed an unusual one. Chicago architect George W. Maher may well have designed the structure with the recent Columbian Exposition in mind, thus bringing to the San Joaquin Valley a bit of its own well-received Spanish imagery. Like all of the first mission-style structures, however, the tower was conservative. Only its tile roof and arched cornice referenced the revival.

88 B. J. S. Cahill, "Design for N. S. G. W. Building," *California Architect and Buildings News,* November 1895.

Bernard J. S. Cahill had emigrated from London in 1888, settling in San Francisco in 1891. His proposal for a Native Sons of the Golden West Building was one of several published in *California Architect and Building News* during 1895. In this instance a Mission Revival design did not win the San Francisco competition. Cahill later assumed the role of architectural theorist and critic in the Bay Area.

88

87

89 Percy and Hamilton, Maria Kip Orphanage, San Francisco, 1896. Perspective published in *California Architect and Building News*, September 1896.

Maria Lawrence Kip had come to San Francisco in 1854 with her husband, Episcopalian Bishop William I. Kip. As one of her charitable contributions to the city, she founded an orphanage. However, it was not until 1896, several years after Mrs. Kip's death, that the institution had the funds to erect its own building—previously the organization was housed at two different city locations.

90 William Binder, Convalescent Cottage, Agnew, 1899. Perspective published in *California Architect and Building News*, February 1899.

San Jose architect William Binder also contributed a Mission Revival institutional design—that for a convalescent cottage on the grounds of the State Hospital for the Insane at Agnew in Santa Clara County.

furthered their work with the Maria Kip orphanage (Fig. 89), while Hermann and Swain designed a similar structure for Thermalito. The imagery employed in cemetery and orphanage design may have been deliberate. Certainly both types were repeatedly executed in the style. By March 1897 Henry Ellington Brook, in *The County and City of Los Angeles*, succinctly stated that "Southern California is a Spanish-American section in its climate, its nomenclature and in its architecture. What is popularly known as the 'Mission style' is the vogue both for homes or for certain classes of public buildings."[36] (Fig. 90)

The success of the California Building at the Columbian Exposition of 1893 and that of the 1894 Midwinter Fair in San Francisco not only fostered the beginnings of a mission style, but also brought forth another round of theoretical discussion. In 1894 the Southern Pacific Company published *California for Health, Pleasure and Profit.* In a section entitled "Influence of Climate," the author noted, "It is *climate* that makes certain features recognized as characteristic of and appropriate to any

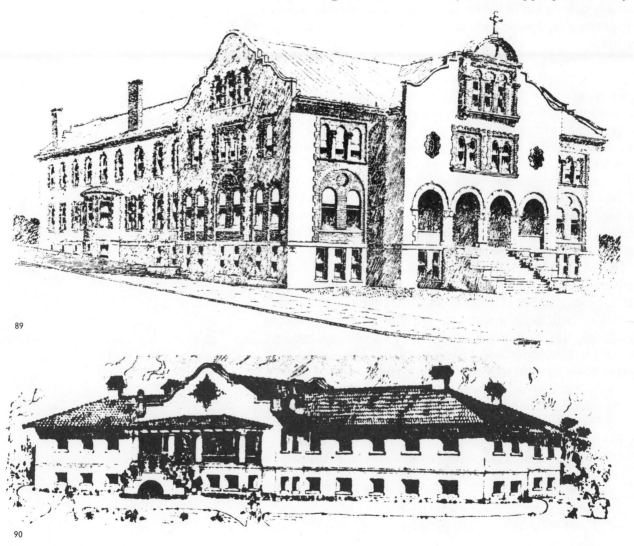

89

90

given section. Even the local architecture . . . depends on the requirements of temperature and weather. In a warm, mild, beneficent climate, homes may be built with consideration toward effects of beauty that could not be indulged in a cold, rigorous region." Differing from the writers of the 1880s, the author referred specifically to mission architecture as the best residential model, interpreting patios, gables, and tile roofs as the result of careful consideration. "The porches and gables and ornamentations that would be uncomfortable and annoying wind-traps in a region of storms and squalls, may be indulged in with impunity and pleasure in a section where reigns calm, equable weather. The bright red roof and gaudy finishings that would look preposterous under the unobstructed glare and in the conventional contrasts of a city street, add to the appearance of beauty and comfort in a rural locality, where the rawness of the color is tempered by juxtaposition with the greens and browns of the luxuriant foliage of a balmy climate."[37] The pamphlet also highlighted California's mission heritage through its mention of the recently formed Landmarks Club.

A mission style went hand in hand with preservation, restoration, and popularization of the missions. Laura Bride Powers commented in her *Story of the Old Missions* of 1893, "I have endeavored to tell their tale of ascendency and ruin . . . to enlist sympathy in the cause of their restoration . . . let us Californians establish our claims to those evidences of stability by preserving our mission ruins from further disintegration." Another pamphlet, *Land of Sunshine*, poignantly encapsulated the changes in sentiment during the 1880s and early 1890s. Its cover jacket juxtaposed a pastoral mission scene with the Moorish-Mission California Building, while the text actively discussed mission restoration. Frank A. Miller, later responsible for Mission Revival enthusiasm in Riverside, was among the businessmen who backed the pamphlet.[38]

The 1893 pamphlet *Land of Sunshine* gave its name, and perhaps even its promotional purpose, to a new journal in June 1894. From the start, California architecture received much attention. With the appointment of Charles Fletcher Lummis as editor in July, theoretical debate occupied center stage. Sumner P. Hunt authored the initial article, "The Adobe in Architecture." For March 1895 Lummis penned "The Lesson of the Adobe." Stressing the practicality of an adobe or pseudo-adobe architecture, he declared that the three lessons offered by the state's architectural heritage were "the non-conducting wall, the patio, the veranda," or—as he restated it—"Comfort, Security, Picturesqueness." Lummis emphasized the attraction of the massive wall: "well, yourself, which would you go the farther to see; any frame house in Los Angeles, or one of these artistic and unhackneyed disciples of the adobe?" Hunt's Froebel Institute in Los Angeles and Roehrig's Stuart

House in Pasadena were featured as the modern mission examples.[39]

Land of Sunshine repeatedly treated the patio and the veranda. In June 1895 Lummis described the patio as an open room appropriate to regional conditions: "build your house around at least three sides of a generous plot, and make that the best . . . if you surround it with long, deep piazzas or real *portales* of Roman arches, like Mission corridors, you will begin to wonder how you ever called the other thing a home." He cited local examples in which the patio was key. Concluding, Lummis—perhaps unconsciously—characterized the suburban ranch house that would later typify Los Angeles County: "the average man will by then ["fifty years hence"] be living in a home

91 Arthur B. Benton, 1911. Portrait published in *Architect and Engineer*, February 1911.

Born in Illinois, Arthur B. Benton began his career as a clerk with the Atchison, Topeka and Santa Fe in Topeka, Kansas. He studied architecture at a local school of design, and then, in 1891, moved to Los Angeles. During the 1890s Benton became associated with Charles Fletcher Lummis. He not only wrote articles on architecture, but also participated in the Landmarks Club. After the turn of the century he designed numerous Mission Revival buildings.

adapted to the country." The following month he analyzed the veranda. "If anyone cares to take a little primary lesson in the art of living, one should go first on a warm summer day and try to fancy that one is happy on the porch of the average redwood box of those we are building here; and then go sit or lounge in a real *portal.* " In August 1897 Arthur B. Benton again stressed the unparalleled qualities of privacy and comfort found in the patio, noting its appropriateness for a California life style. A prominent Los Angeles architect practicing in the Mission Revival, Benton was also actively involved in preservation.[40] (Fig. 91)

As secretary of the Southern California Chapter of the American Institute of Architects, Benton used *Land of Sunshine* to endorse a mission style. Others followed his lead. In 1896 R. B. Dickinson, in his *Los Angeles of Today Architecturally,* asserted, "California has not . . . as yet developed a characteristic architecture of its own; but that it is fast reaching that point . . . seems probable . . . the tendency . . . seems to be towards . . . such features . . . as are best calculated to produce a picturesque effect, and . . . the advantages of sunshine and view." The patio, arcade, gable, tower, and tile roof fulfilled this prophecy. Miscellaneous articles appeared after 1896. In December 1898 Caroline L. Overman wrote for *House Beautiful,* "The result has been that after experimenting with everything from Swiss chalets to Colonial mansions, the architects of the Southwest have decided that the best type of building for this frostless, sunshiny land is the kind that has already been there for several hundred years. The number of modern Spanish buildings in California is not yet large, but they are so conspicuously suitable that future builders must follow so excellent an example." Between 1900 and 1910 national architectural journals took up the discussion, patterning many articles after those which had been published in *Land of Sunshine.*[41]

Lummis had mentioned the renewed interest in preservation in his editorial section, "In the Lion's Den," in December 1895. During the previous year he had organized the Landmarks Club, concentrating on Missions San Juan Capistrano, San Fernando, San Diego, and Pala. The club was as much a promotional organization as it was a restoration agency. Among the original members of the board of directors were Lummis, Hunt, and Benton, with an Advisory Board including Colonel Harrison Gray Otis, Tessa L. Kelso, Chas. Cassat Davis, Charles Dwight Willard, and Elmer Wachtel. The composition was especially noteworthy. Otis was the publisher of the *Times.* Kelso had led preservation efforts in the 1880s. Davis was president of the Los Angeles Board of Education and had written an article on Hunt's Froebel Institute. Willard wrote for the Los Angeles Chamber of Commerce. Wachtel was an artist known for his etchings of the missions.[42]

In 1896 and 1897 *American Architect and Building News* canvassed the work of the Landmarks Club. The journal observed, "Simultaneously with the effort to perpetuate the style embodied in these buildings, a movement has been made looking to the conservation of such of the fabrics of these buildings as yet remain, as monuments of the early history of California." In the *Overland Monthly* of January 1897, P. N. Boeringer also linked mission design with reverence for their historic models. "Looking at it from a purely artistic and architectural standpoint the Missions should certainly be preserved. There is no other style of architecture so fitting in a California landscape . . . The gingerbread buildings of our summer and winter resorts do not fit our landscape." Continuing, he commented that "The lover of the beautiful . . . will sigh for a Mission renaissance and as certainly will the renaissance be an accomplished fact." Charles Fletcher Lummis was later to assess the correlative nature of preservation and the Mission Revival. "The influence of the Landmarks Club was felt in many less obvious ways. Not often do we see, in other parts of the land, a home or building done in the old New England style. But for each one such, there are a thousand of the 'Mission architecture' today."[43] During the late 1890s, the Mission Revival and mission preservation surged forward together. Promotionalism shadowed both.

Chapter Four

The Mission Revival Comes of Age

Romanesque is grand, yes; Gothic is very spiritual,
that's true; but give me neither Romanesque nor Gothic;
much less Italian Renaissance, and least of all English Colonial
—this is California—give me Mission.

Felix Rey, "A Tribute to Mission Style," *Architect and Engineer*, October 1924

92

Just prior to the turn of the century, L. Clare Davis observed for the Stockton *Mail* that although the Mission Revival was still infrequently seen, there would soon be "a rush for mission buildings." And what a rush it was. In 1906 Sarah Comstock discussed the style for *American Homes and Gardens*. The Mission Revival had generated "a wonderful and beautiful array of 'Mission' houses. . .now the typical homes of the Golden State." Residential trend-setting provided the cutting edge. "The great majority of the wealthy home makers of California are building in this style, and spending in that building sums that would make the old Padres gasp could they see whither their example has led. Los Angeles . . . shows Mission homes on every residence street. The famous Orange Grove Avenue of Pasadena, that Mecca of midwinter summer seekers, is lined with these modern 'Dobes.' " Writers described entire cities as blossoming in "this gay style of building."[1] (Fig. 92)

An ambivalence, however, did exist among clients and architects. What was proper for the Mission Revival? As had been true in the 1890s, opinions were often polarized. Excess or frugality? Ornament or simplicity? Both were tied to a mission style. Giving the views of two anonymous architects, Comstock presented the dichotomy. "One San Francisco architect has entered a protest against the introduction of Moorish elaboration in the modern buildings, and has designed several houses according to the rigid severity of the simplest Missions . . . An opposing architect says, 'So long as we imitate all the beauties of the Padres' building, why should we not add the lavishness of adornment that wealth now makes possible?' " As Comstock concluded, flamboyance was more popular. Austerity, however, remained an undercurrent—one which linked the Mission Revival to the modern movement. Herbert D. Croly commented for *Architect and Engineer* in 1906, "Rudimentary as these buildings [the missions] were and simple to the verge of attenuation, they reached, both by what they avoided, and by what they effected the essentials of good domestic architecture." The massive volumetric effect and neutral coloration of the missions made them an ideal model for an architecture of planar wall surfaces, one which could be dissociated with revivalism. For several Southern California

92 William Helm House, Fresno, 1901-02. (J. W. Snyder: 1980)
The Helm House in Fresno was one of the first mission style residences for the San Joaquin Valley. Built for the Helm family, area settlers and major land holders, the house featured a gable with quatrefoil on the main facade.

architects, notably Irving Gill, the Mission Revival was a stepping stone away from the notion of dependence upon past styles.[2]

The Mission Revival quickly became popular for apartments and low-cost, made-to-order bungalows. Although functionally inappropriate for multi-story, multi-occupant urban buildings, the style nonetheless gave the middle-class citizen the opportunity to live in a distinctively Californian residence. Gardens, wrought-iron balconies, tile roofs, stucco ornament—all made the rectangular apartment block attractive to the newcomer. (Fig. 93) The Mission Revival offered the tenant the flavor of an "olden time" and of a foreign culture, yet also allowed him familiar standardized conveniences. In several instances roof gardens further enhanced the appeal. It was the inexpensive, easily fabricated concrete bungalow, however, that assured the Mission Revival's popularity as a residential style. Engineers and contractors published numerous manuals of bungalow and cottage craft. (Fig. 94) In a sense, these were twentieth-century pattern books, providing the layman with rudimentary elevations and plans. A dream house could be chosen for a moderate price. Special requests were made to order, and businessmen fully realized the monetary potential of "Mission Revival for the masses." (Fig. 95) In at least one instance, a member of the Los Angeles Chamber of Commerce was directly involved in the distribution of such mail-order plans. Simultaneously, articles on the bungalow appeared in *Architect and Engineer.* The Mission Revival was thought by some to best fulfill the dynamics of "the low, spacious, airy house." It was a type ideal "where the ground is comparatively cheap and the

93 J. Cather Newsom/A. W. Smith, Casa Rosa Apartments, Oakland, 1909. Published in *Architect and Engineer,* September 1909. [Demolished]

The Casa Rosa Apartments in Oakland of 1909 present a dilemma of attribution. Firmly credited to Oakland architect A. W. Smith by *Architect and Engineer* in 1909, these same apartments are discussed at length as the work of another Oakland architect, J. Cather Newsom, in *Greater Oakland* of 1911. Identical illustrations appear with both. In fact, the Casa Rosa Apartments do resemble other Newsom designs, recalling most especially that for the Gilroy Town Hall of 1905 by brother Samuel.

94 Jacob A. Knapp, ''Sketch for a Mission Cottage,'' *California Architect and Building News,* May 1899.

As early as 1899, *California Architect and Building News* presented a prototype for a mission cottage. Jacob A. Knapp's design was really for a very simple bungalow translated into the idiom of the Mission Revival. It was for the middle class, and thus was altogether different from the mansions designed sporadically during the preceding years. Predictably, the open veranda was a key feature.

95 L. M. Turton, ''Design for a Mission Bungalow,'' elevation published in *Architect and Engineer,* October 1910.

By 1910 the Mission Revival bungalow was widespread. Napa architect L. M. Turton offered his design for client W. J. Lindow. The bungalow could have been for nearly anyone, anywhere. Its tile roof, repetitive gables, oversized quatrefoils, partially enclosed porch, and pergola were to be seen in cities and towns throughout the West and Southwest—and oftentimes in other parts of the country as well.

93

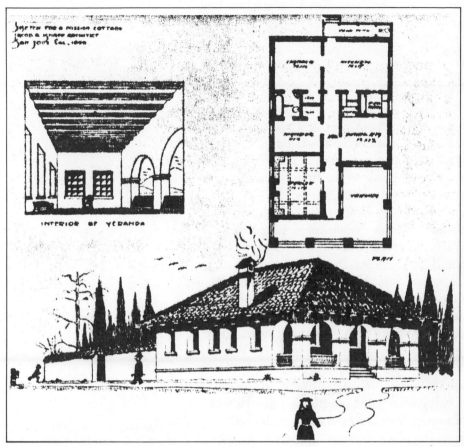

94

FRONT ELEVATION

95

climate is such that a court filled with flowers and a building permitting of unlimited ventilation would be a delight." Mission remained a favorite, leaving a legacy for the subdivisions of today.[3] (Fig. 96)

Planners also applied the Mission Revival to entire communities. Certainly, businessmen backing the boom towns of Sierra Madre, Alhambra, Altadena, San Juan Capistrano, and San Rafael Heights intended that the style attract future buyers. (Fig. 97) In 1911, *Architect and Engineer* heralded Planada, nine miles east of Merced, as California's "model municipality." "The architecture of the city will be along the Spanish mission lines, and the residences will be typical bungalows." In 1915, and again in 1916, the Garden City Company of California published *Ideal Homes in Garden Communities*, suggesting that the Mission Revival was best for California's "garden cities." And in 1917-19 the New Cornelia Copper Company and the Phelps-Dodge Corporation commissioned Kenyon and Maine and Bertram G. Goodhue, respectively, to design company mining towns at Ajo, Arizona, and Tyrone, New Mexico. Both communities were by-products of the national campaign for industrial housing generated during the First World War. Ajo displayed the full array of Mission Revival accents, while Tyrone offered a peculiar mixture of extremely simple Spanish-Pueblo Revival housing and early Spanish Colonial Revival public buildings. In more restricted projects, such civic improvement was taking place throughout the West and Southwest. Pasadena, Riverside, and Santa Barbara were heavily missionized.[4] (Fig. 98-101)

96 Mission Revival bungalow, Palo Alto, c. 1912-14. (K. J. Weitze: 1977)

Again combining the Mission Revival and Craftsman aesthetics, this Palo Alto bungalow also featured a mission-style garage.

96

97

98

97 Arthur B. Benton, residence, San Juan Capistrano, c. 1910. (K. J. Weitze: 1978)

Benton's residence for a patron in San Juan Capistrano fit the Mission Revival pattern. Plain stucco walls, simplified gable, and veranda accented the two-story structure.

98 Burnham and Bleisner, Carnegie Library, Riverside, 1903. Published in *American Builders Review*, December 1905. [Demolished]

99 Exchange Building, Riverside, c. 1911. Published in *Architect and Engineer*, August 1911.

99

100

101

In 1910 the editor of *American Architect and Building News* remarked, "If there is a section of the United States which possesses a style in its residential work that section is undisputably the Southern Coast of California. Its distinctive manner of building and designing has a legitimate origin in the Spanish traditions of the old local missions and was developed therefrom in accordance with climatic and topographical conditions and modern needs and improvements." The Southern Pacific, too, characterized the region as a desert that had become a garden, "the beautiful solitude populous with homes." Continuing, the author declared "there is a great desire to perpetuate the structures which once were exotics, but now are part of the history of the land." By 1939 one writer estimated that over a million Mission Revival residences had been built in this section of California alone.[5]

Mission Revival also offered much for the railroads. The Santa Fe expanded tracks into California between 1881 and 1896, while the Southern Pacific laid 4,500 miles of rail to California and within the state between 1887 and 1910. Both lines were thoroughly immersed in regional promotionalism: a mission style furnished appropriate imagery for the depots. In

100 Union Pacific depot, Riverside, 1904. (J. W. Snyder: 1978)

101 American Fruit Growers Incorporated, warehouse, Riverside, 1912. (J. W. Snyder: 1978)
Citywide Mission Revival imagery was not uncommon, especially in Southern California. In Riverside a mission-style library, exchange building, Union Pacific depot, and warehouse were only a few of the municipality's buildings working together to create the Spanish atmosphere so popular with both the newcomer and the tourist.

the first decade of the twentieth century, other railway companies also launched a depot-building program. Between 1900 and 1920 Mission Revival became the style not only for California stations, but also for depots erected throughout the Southwest. (Fig. 102-104) *Architect and Engineer* and *Inland Architect and News Record* carried numerous illustrations, noting

102

103

102 Northwestern Pacific depot, Petaluma, 1914. (J. W. Snyder: 1980)

103 Las Vegas and Tonopah depot, Rhyolite, Nevada, 1907-08. (Nevada Historical Society, Reno)

104 Harvey L. Page, International and Great Northern depot, San Antonio, Texas, 1907. (K. J. Weitze: 1978)

Mission Revival depots appeared on nearly every railroad line in the West and Southwest during the 1905-15 period. They were of varied scale and type; some were urban, some rural. Perhaps San Antonio's International and Great Northern depot, designed by Harvey L. Page, best epitomizes rail mission imagery at its height. Page adapted elements of other popular trends of the period, including Beaux-Arts central dome and Greek-cross plan, combining these with mission gables, tile accents, and quatrefoils. Page, a San Antonio architect, also included corporate imagery: a detailed IG&N logo in the stained glass of the oversized quatrefoils. Most unusual, however, was the inexplicable American Indian perched high atop the dome.

104

that, as with residential architecture, a mission style was admirably suited to the climate and heritage of the region. And as Arthur B. Benton proclaimed in 1911, "no better advertisers" existed.[6]

In 1900 the Southern Pacific observed, "These monuments of a century past [the missions] are so conveniently located near the railroads that to pass them by were in the tourist inexcusable." Drawing an analogy between modern depots and the historic mission way stations, it continued, "The Franciscan friars journeying northward from San Diego a century and a quarter ago made their trail almost as the way now is of the Southern Pacific." Southern Pacific's Architectural Bureau designed mission stations for Davis, Berkeley, San Francisco, Modesto, Visalia, Porterville, and Santa Barbara. (Fig. 105-107) Two other depots also prominent during the early twentieth-century, were erected in San Antonio, Texas, and Tuscon, Arizona. (Fig. 108) *Sunset* acknowledged J. D. Isaacs and D. J. Patterson as company architects for many of these stations. Southern Pacific depots were closely patterned after the missions, employing a pastiche of bell towers, gables, and arches. Exemplifying the railway's interest in the Mission Revival, W. H. Wheeler—a representative from the company's engineering department—devoted one quarter of a 1906 lecture on architectural styles to a discussion of historic and modern mission design. Wheeler gave the lecture before the Hillside Club in Berkeley.[7]

The Santa Fe also commissioned many Mission Revival depots. A promotional pamphlet of 1901, *The San Joaquin*

105

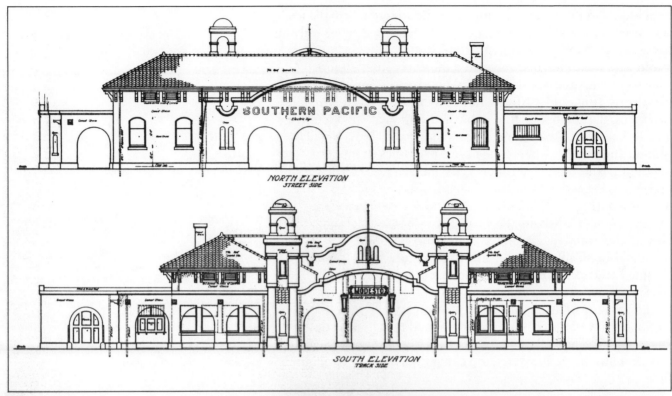

SOUTHERN PACIFIC

NORTH ELEVATION
STREET SIDE

SOUTH ELEVATION
TRACK SIDE

106

107

105 Southern Pacific depot, Berkeley, 1913. (California Department of Transportation: 1939)

106 Southern Pacific depot, Modesto, 1914, elevation. (Public Utilities Commission Record Group, California State Archives, Office of the Secretary of State, Sacramento)

107 Francis Wilson, Southern Pacific depot, Santa Barbara, 1905. (J. W. Snyder: 1979)

108 J. D. Isaacs and D. J. Patterson, Southern Pacific depot, San Antonio, Texas, 1902. (K. J. Weitze: 1978)
The Southern Pacific Company promoted the mission image most heavily in California, although it did extend the station type to major southwestern cities on cross-country lines. In particular, the well-traveled Sunset Route from New Orleans to Los Angeles was riddled with mission-style depots. After the turn of the century, the Southern Pacific and the Mission Revival were coincident wherever tourism and immigration were expected.

108

Valley, illustrated stations at Bakersfield, Tulare, Visalia, Stockton and Fresno. Each emphasized horizontal roof planes and simple arches. Major entrances were designed repeatedly in imitation of the two-towered mission church. Often a large gable with quatrefoil inset accented the entry. In the more lavish complexes a Mission Revival hotel or restaurant adjoined the depot. (Fig. 109-110) Charles F. Whittlesey, a Los Angeles architect, designed the often-published station at Albuquerque in 1905. *Architect and Engineer* characterized the New Mexico station and hotel as "one of the purest examples of modern mission architecture." Architects designed large-scale depots for Ash Fork, Arizona; Trinidad, Colorado; and San Diego, California. (Fig. 111-112) In 1913, *Architectural Review* described Santa Fe Mission Revival railway hotels as among the best of their kind in the United States and Europe.[8]

Two other California railroads, the Western Pacific and the Pacific Electric, were among those that erected stations. The Western Pacific began construction in Oakland in 1906, building many of its depots in the mission style. Pacific Electric of Southern California, too, commissioned many such stations, between 1908 and 1914.[9] Most particularly, Western Pacific's Sacramento depot illustrated the company's building program.

109 W. H. Mohr, Santa Fe depot and eating house, San Bernardino, 1916. (Public Utilities Commission Record Group, California State Archives, Office of the Secretary of State, Sacramento)

110 Charles F. Whittlesey, Santa Fe eating house, Merced, 1908. Published in *Architect and Engineer*, March 1908.

Oftentimes the Atchison, Topeka and Santa Fe commissioned depots that were in fact depot-complexes, with not just station, but also restaurant and hotel. As was the case at Merced—just south of Stockton in the San Joaquin Valley—the typical station often had a Harvey House. Fred Harvey's restaurants accompanied the tourist on his journey with the Santa Fe. One of the later Mission Revival depots, at San Bernardino, was also one of the most lavish. It offered the traveling public the full array of services.

109

110

111 Harrison Albright, Santa Fe depot and hotel, Ash Fork, Arizona, 1906. Perspective published in *Architect and Engineer*, February 1906. [Demolished c. 1973]

The immense depot for the Santa Fe in Ash Fork, Arizona, was one of Harrison Albright's first commissions received in Los Angeles. (Prior to 1905 Albright had established a successful practice in Charleston.) The Santa Fe had made no mistake in hiring Albright: the mission image was one intended to make the Santa Fe line an even more attractive lure West.

112 Bakewell and Brown, Santa Fe depot, San Diego, 1914. Photograph and plan in Henry C. Smith, *Public Buildings, Banks, Transportation Terminals*, loose-leaf binder, College of Environmental Design Library, University of California, Berkeley.

Designed to coincide with the Panama California International Exposition of 1915, Santa Fe's formal Mission Revival depot complemented San Diego's elaborate fair grounds at Balboa Park. Bakewell and Brown, a San Francisco firm, were busy with another prominent mission-style complex during this time as well—the later phase of buildings for Stanford University.

111

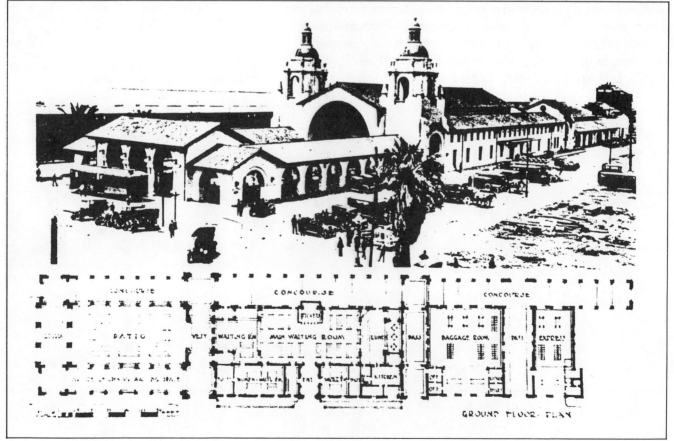

112

(Fig. 113) Willis Polk and Company, the West Coast branch office of D. H. Burnham and Company, designed the 1910 station. The walls exhibited a planar quality that worked well with an overall horizontality. Polk continued to be intrigued by the missions, designing further Mission Revival buildings, and becoming active in the preservation of San Francisco's Mission Dolores.[10]

Following the late 1880s boom in Southern California, vacationers flocked West, stimulating the commissioning of hotels as they had of railroad stations. The typical Mission Revival hotel featured two towers, first-story—and sometimes second-story—arcaded promenades, tile roofs, and mixed fenestration. In many cases, a U-shaped courtyard was a part of the plan, providing a pseudo-patio for guests. A rectangular vertical block with uniform room arrangement often remained a necessity, even though this scheme was the antithesis of that of the missions. Yet, antithesis or no, the Mission Revival hotel was widely popular, exuding an atmosphere of festivity reminiscent of the earlier expositions.

Promoters commissioned three such hotels in Pasadena alone before 1903: the Green, the Maryland, and the Raymond. (Fig. 114) Additions to the Green, construction of the Maryland, and, finally, completion of the Raymond each illustrated the Mission Revival's competitive edge. Imitating the format of the Green, each hotel superimposed two center towers and minimal arcading onto the older rectangular block. Similar published hotels of the period included ones at Paso Robles (1902), Los Angeles (1902), Long Beach (1906), Byron Hot

113 Willis Polk, Western Pacific depot, Sacramento, 1910. Perspective published in *Architect and Engineer*, January 1912.

Working as the West Coast representative of D. H. Burnham and Company of Chicago, Willis Polk designed the Mission Revival depot for Western Pacific at Sacramento in 1910. Polk had worked in Burnham's office just after the turn of the century and had remained a close friend and associate. The Sacramento depot was one of the later commissions to bear the stamp of D. H. Burnham and Company—even, if here, indirectly. Daniel H. Burnham died in 1912.

114 Second annex, Hotel Green, Pasadena, 1903. Perspective published in Pasadena Board of Trade, *Illustrated Souvenir Book*, Pasadena, 1903. (The Bancroft Library) [Strange and Carnicle, remodeling and addition, 1891-92, and Frederick L. Roehrig, Raymond Avenue connecting arch, 1898, demolished in 1935]

The full-scale Hotel Green summarized events of 1888-1903. Begun as a promotional scheme in conjunction with the nearby Santa Fe depot, the hotel witnessed some initial setbacks following the dry post-boom years. Then with the Spanish addition of 1891 and Santa Fe's California Special of the same year, business picked up. But it was 1893, with yet another Santa Fe-advertised route and the enthusiasm for California generated by the Columbian Exposition, that brought the surge towards a climax. Roehrig's lavish Spanish annex of 1898 with a porte-cochere that directly accommodated the Santa Fe, foreshadowed the final planned design of 1903. After the turn of the century, the large-scale Mission Revival tourist hotel had arrived.

113

114

Springs (1907), Stockton (1908), and Santa Rosa (1907). [11] (Fig. 115) The Hotel Stockton was a somewhat unique case: architect E.B. Brown drew upon an 1899 design by Charles Beasley for the commission. [12] (Fig. 116-117) In 1906 Charles F. Whittlesey designed the Hotel Wentworth (Fig. 118) in the

115 Austin and Brown, Bixby Hotel, Long Beach, 1906. Perspective published in *Architect and Engineer*, April 1906. [Demolished]

Austin and Brown's Bixby Hotel in Long Beach achieved national noteriety during its construction in 1906. Published in April, and described as one of the world's largest reinforced concrete structures, the Bixby partially collapsed in early November. Knowledgeable engineers, including San Francisco's John B. Leonard, immediately examined the debris. They faulted the contractors for misunderstanding the properties of reinforced concrete. Austin and Brown were absolved of blame for the incident, and the Bixby was rebuilt.

116 E. B. Brown, Hotel Stockton, Stockton, 1908. (K. J. Weitze: 1979)

117 Charles Beasley, ''Suggested Plans for a Big Hotel,'' Stockton *Mail*, December 20, 1899. (California State Library, Sacramento)

E. B. Brown's Hotel Stockton was one of the most elaborate Mission Revival hotels in central California. And in many ways, it was one of the earliest. Architect Charles Beasley had proposed a mission-style hotel for the city location in 1899, following with other similar proposals in 1900 and 1906. By 1908 Stockton architect E. B. Brown finally designed the much-discussed hotel, borrowing ideas both directly and indirectly from Beasley's earlier proposals.

115

116

117

Mission Revival, again for Pasadena, while Santa Barbara showcased the Hotel Potter. (Fig. 119) In other areas of the Southwest, notably Texas, it was popular to replace the tower with a simplified gable reminiscent of the Alamo. The St. Anthony in San Antonio (1909) and the Galvez in Galveston (1911) exemplify this trend. (Fig. 120) Again a readily identifiable mission detail served to make the association for the vacationer.[13]

Arthur B. Benton pioneered a more flamboyant style in the

118

118 Charles F. Whittlesey, Hotel Wentworth, Pasadena, 1906. Elevation published in *Architect and Engineer*, March 1908.

Pasadena quickly became a mecca of Mission Revival resort hotels. In the twentieth century such hostelries exceeded everyone's imagination. Whittlesey's Hotel Wentworth not only showcased sheer size, but it also showcased new technology. Whittlesey had been trained in the Chicago office of Louis Sullivan during the 1890s and then had become chief architect for the Santa Fe. By 1905 he had achieved major design success with reinforced concrete, attracting the attention of German architects and engineers with his Temple Auditorium in Los Angeles. The Wentworth followed the auditorium directly.

119 John Austin, Hotel Potter, Santa Barbara, 1901. California Wheelmen, Good Roads Tour, 1912. (California Department of Transportation) [Destroyed by fire, 1921]

Designed by John Austin, Santa Barbara's Hotel Potter was yet another illustration of the Mission Revival's popular appeal. Speculators had purchased the land in the 1880s, setting it aside for resort development. Yet it was not until Milo Milton Potter built his hostelry in 1901 that the property achieved its destiny. Entrepreneur Potter had owned and managed previous hotels in Los Angeles and Florida.

119

120 J. Flood Walker, Hotel St. Anthony, San Antonio, Texas, 1909. Published in *American Architect and Building News*, September 1909.

Los Angeles architect J. Flood Walker applied a mission style to the traditional multi-story downtown hotel in his design for the St. Anthony. Here only mission gable capping the seventh story carried the revival imagery.

Mission Inn of Riverside, 1902-14. (Fig. 121-122) Frank Miller, businessman and promoter, commissioned Benton to design additions to his late nineteenth-century hotel. Laid out to resemble a mission quadrangle—with arcades, one-story wings, decorative gables, and gateways—the inn was dubbed "a modern Alhambra" and "first of all, Californian." The Mission Inn, with its Mission (1902), Cloister (1910), and Spanish (1914) wings, was the most conspicuously elaborate, and, thereafter, the most widely published, of the Mission Revival hotels. Myron Hunt, Elmer Grey, and Stanley Wilson collaborated with Benton on its design. Inside, Arts and Crafts mission furniture enhanced the effect. Miller continued to add more promotional gimmicks as the years passed. A Mission Play, patterned after the Passion Play of Oberammergau, attracted crowds of visitors annually from 1912 through 1928.[14]

Benton designed another Mission Revival hotel in 1911, the Arlington in Santa Barbara. (Fig. 123-124) It was grandiose, but unusual. Most Mission Revival architects, including Benton, did not draw upon specific missions for their inspiration; rather they relied upon adaptations of a typological category such as "gables." In the Arlington, however, Benton mirrored the facades of San Juan Capistrano, San Luis Rey, San Antonio de Padua, Santa Barbara, and San Diego. Two wings of the hotel even reflected the peculiar buttressing from Mission San Gabriel. Writing about the influence of the missions for *Architect and Engineer* that same year, the architect reflected, "Our Mission hotels are proving how great the demand by tourists for something 'different' from the conventional." Certainly this was true for the Arlington. Its grounds included a "jungle," "servants' social hall," "curio shop," tennis courts, gardens, fountain, auto park, and picturesque drives.[15]

Myron Hunt and Elmer Grey continued this approach to the Mission Revival, designing residences and hotels for wealthy clients. Grey's Beverly Hills Hotel of 1910-11 followed the Benton pattern. Recalling a Hollywood set, the Mission Inn, the Arlington, and the Beverly Hills established the stereotype. Although not always the chosen style, the Mission Revival was often among the prime choices for expensive tourist hotels built

121

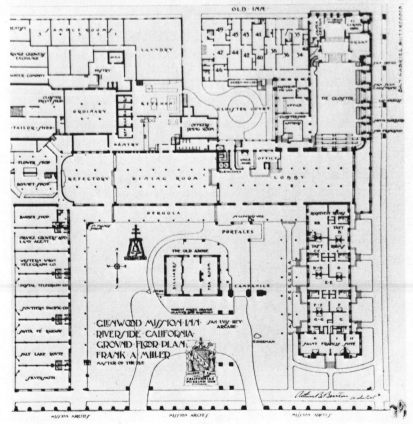

122

121-122 Benton, Hunt, Grey, and Wilson, Mission Inn, Riverside, 1902-14. Courtyard and plan published in *Architect and Engineer*, February 1911.

The queen of the Mission Revival hotels was the Mission Inn in Riverside. Backed by local businessman Frank Miller, the inn played to the tourist's every notion. Architects Benton, Hunt, Grey, and Wilson included all the appropriate mission details in the successive additions commissioned between 1902 and 1914. Streetside shops included a predictable group: orange growers and land agents, Western Union Telegram, Postal Telegraph, Southern Pacific, Santa Fe, and Salt Lake Route all maintained offices here. Again the tourist and potential immigrant-investor were the clientele sought.

123

124

123-124 Arthur B. Benton, Arlington Hotel, Santa Barbara, 1910. Perspective and plan published in *Architect and Engineer,* February 1911. [Destroyed by earthquake, 1925]

Benton designed another flamboyant mission-style hotel for Santa Barbara in 1910. Like the Mission Inn, the complex of buildings and grounds catered to tourism. The hotel occupied an entire city block.

in California during the first fifteen years of the twentieth century. Even Berkeley's Claremont Hotel elicited a mission design in its competition: William Knowles, an architect active in preservation issues, again demonstrated the influence of the Mission Inn and of the California Building. (Fig. 125) An amalgam of tourist and exposition architecture, Knowles's design epitomizes this type of Mission Revival hotel.[16]

Although architects interpreted the Mission Revival for residential, railway, and hotel architecture, it was California schools that absorbed their attention most thoroughly. In 1929 Steven McGroarty pronounced in his *Mission Memories*: "I think that our schools of today architecturally are the logical outcome of the missions." Felix Rey wrote for *Architect and Engineer*: "Even of themselves the simple Mission forms calm mind and heart; but if the story of our early Missions is once well imparted to the children of a well-designed Mission-style school and the derivation of its forms pointed out, those forms and the memory of them will keep that story in their minds for life." The Mission Revival eclipsed all other styles as the one most appropriate for both Northern and Southern California's elementary, secondary, and advanced educational facilities. "Said a certain pastor very emphatically to his architect after having discussed with him the various styles of architecture in order to select one for his new school: 'Romanesque is grand, yes; Gothic is very spiritual, that's true; but give me neither Romanesque nor Gothic; much less Italian Renaissance, and least of all English Colonial—this is California—give me Mission.'"[17]

As with other types of buildings, architects designed Mission Revival schools extensively from 1900 through 1915. From the very first years, 'mission' was intimately tied to changes in educational philosophy. A trustee in Stockton proclaimed in

125 William Knowles, ''Competitive Design for Tourist Hotel at Claremont Park, Berkeley,'' *Architect and Engineer*, April 1906.

Perhaps if Berkeley had been located in Southern California, Knowles's proposal for a large-scale Mission Revival hotel might have been accepted. Instead C. W. Dickey's Craftsman Tudor design was the one preferred for the Claremont.

125

October 1899 that "a Moorish (or old Spanish) schoolhouse would be a distinct and striking improvement upon the architecture of any existing schoolhouse" in the city. The school board did indeed adopt a Spanish style, citing aesthetic, health, and safety rationales to support their choice. At the turn of the century, Mission Revival schools were still very few. M. Hume, in *Los Angeles Architecturally* of 1902, illustrated the Twentieth Street School House, while *Architectural Record* published Arthur B. Benton's Harvard School, in Los Angeles of 1905. Mission-style schools typically featured an oversized front gable, centered between two towers. Tile roof, patio, and arcade were standard. Although a gable might not overshadow the towers, it was this motif that appeared most frequently. It was generally recognized that one-story buildings represented the ideal, although schools two to three stories were still acceptable and to be preferred over the traditional multi-story type that incorporated no patio, arcades, or indoor-outdoor space. In cases where either budget or spatial requirements did not allow the inclusion of a courtyard, the architect designed a commonplace vertical block school with a tower or gables superimposed upon the facade. Architect J. Lee Burton's design for a 1906 school in Long Beach is indicative of this approach.[18]

Prominent California architects were among those designers noted for Mission Revival schools. B. G. McDougall and William H. Weeks entered the field of school design early. McDougall had worked with his father during the Columbian Exposition and Midwinter Fair competitions of the early 1890s. By 1906 he had designed schools for Visalia, Fresno, and Porterville. (Fig. 126) School boards also commissioned William H. Weeks for numerous mission-style schools between 1906 and 1915. *Architect and Engineer* discussed Weeks as having designed "as many, if not more, high-class school buildings in California than any other architect." The journal published his Mission Revival designs for San Luis Obispo, Watsonville, Gustine, Hollister (Fig. 127), King City, Glenn County, Monterey, and Paso Robles.[19] In 1908-10 Myron Hunt and Elmer Grey collaborated on the Throop Polytechnic Institute in Pasadena, rendering a lavish mission plan. (Fig. 128) Irving Gill designed the Bishop's School for Girls at La Jolla in 1909, while Frank S. Allen of Pasadena designed institutions for National City, Banning, Redlands, Pasadena, and San Jose. (Fig. 129-132) During these same years, architects Louis S. Stone, Henry C. Smith, Walter H. Parker, and John J. Donovan initiated the adoption of mission design in Northern California.[20] (Fig. 133-136)

Several architects spoke about the appropriateness of the style for California. In 1908 Frank S. Allen evaluated the "mission type school house" for *Architect and Engineer*, commenting that the low, one-to-two-story Mission Revival

126

127

128

126 B.G. McDougall, grammar school, Porterville, c.1903-06. Perspective published in *Architect and Engineer*, June 1906. [Demolished]

127 William H. Weeks, San Benito County High School, Hollister, c. 1911. Published in *Architect and Engineer*, June 1911.
Both McDougall's and Weeks's school designs were typical for the revival. The Porterville school, however, did have one unusual element—its stone masonry construction. Most mission schools were stucco on lath or reinforced concrete.

128 Hunt and Grey, Throop Polytechnic Institute, Pasadena, 1908. Published in *American Architect and Building News*, June 22, 1910. [Remodeled]
Hunt and Grey designed numerous Mission Revival buildings in Pasadena, most for wealthy clients. The Throop Polytechnic Institute reflected this fact once again with a staid scheme that was both mission and Beaux-Arts.

129 Irving Gill, Bishop's School for Girls, La Jolla, 1909. Published in *Concrete-Cement Age*, June 1914.
Best known for his abstractly simple design work with reinforced concrete, Irving Gill certainly approached the Mission Revival from his particular perspective. Yet even Gill incorporated rows of arcades and a mission bell tower in the Bishop's School for Girls design.

129

130 Frank S. Allen, Madison School, Pasadena, 1905. Published in *Architect and Engineer*, September 1908.

Constructed at a cost of $33,000, Madison School was one of a number of structures erected during the Pasadena building boom of 1904-05. Allen, a noted California school architect, designed many Mission Revival institutions throughout California and Arizona.

131-132 Frank S. Allen, school, National City, c.1908. Published in *Architect and Engineer*, September 1908.

Allen's National City school was often published—and often praised—as nearly perfect. Its ground-hugging form, spread over the site, as well as its enclosed courtyard with surrounding arcades, captured the philosophy behind the revival's institutional acceptance. Arch-framed viewsheds also epitomized the inspirational values felt to be closely allied with a mission-style school.

130

131

132

school incorporated principles of earthquake proofing and student safety. Continuing in 1909, Allen recognized the compatibility of a mission style and a healthy educational environment. "Many buildings . . . are now patterned after the ideas of the Mission fathers. This is particularly true of the public schools which, with their large rooms and the necessity of wide and extensive passages lend themselves most admirably to this manner of building." Architect Walter H. Parker included two illustrations of mission-style institutions in a 1910 article on the general requirements of the well-planned school. Implicit was the assumption that good design and the Mission Revival were synonymous.[21]

By 1910 architects were citing climate, quality of light, extensive open spaces, educational requirements, and structural mechanics as sound reasons for the erection of Mission Revival schools. In analyzing the Throop Polytechnic Institute in Pasadena and Pomona College in Pomona, Myron Hunt and Elmer Grey perceived that it was not the decorative

133

134

133 Stone and Smith, grammar school, Modesto, 1906. (McHenry Museum, Modesto) [Demolished]
A somewhat whimsical Mission Revival design, the Modesto schoolhouse featured highly stylized quatrefoils, hooded windows and squat center tower. Originally Stone and Smith submitted an English Tudor design for the school—even publishing their Tudor drawings in *Architect and Engineer* of 1906. How and why the final selection of a Mission Revival design evolved remains an anomaly of the commission.

134 Stone and Smith, Los Gatos High School, Los Gatos, c. 1908. Perspective published in *Architect and Engineer*, December 1908. [Heavily remodeled]

appeal of a mission style that merited attention, but rather the design elements that best adapted themselves to a progressive California educational scene. "It is not intended that the architecture shall necessarily be Mission in style, but the men who designed the California Missions appreciated so thoroughly the peculiar climatic conditions of California that the buildings they built cannot but be an inspiration for succeeding generations. By using intelligently their roof color, their roof materials

135

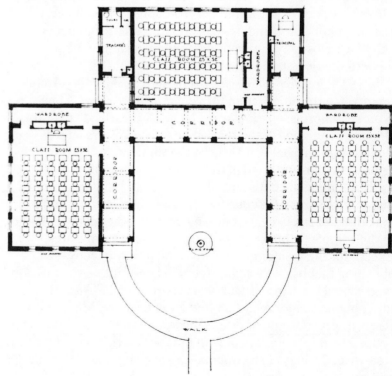

135-136 Walter H. Parker, ''Design for a 3-Room Rural School Building,'' *Architect and Engineer,* March 1910.

Two additional school designs, one built and one proposed, illustrate the range of Mission Revival types. Stone and Smith's Los Gatos High School of c. 1908 recalled the more conservative multi-story institution, while Parker's design for a 3-room rural school building again evoked the principles of a healthy indoor-outdoor atmosphere achieved through courtyards and arcades.

136

and forms, their heavy buttresses with lighter walls between, their strength of masonry and light-colored plastic wall surfaces, the contemporary California architect can perhaps secure the spirit and movement of their best work." In 1911 William H. Weeks again noted the adaptability of the Mission Revival for schools. "This type is peculiarly adapted to California, both in respect to climate and environment. The Mission type of school is necessarily low, and where there is ample ground area a one or two-story school house is preferable to a three or four-story structure."[22]

Even the state government sanctioned mission-style schools. The Department of Instruction published *School Architecture* in 1909, including references to the style. Department writers characterized Frank S. Allen's National City High School as "one of the best examples in the state of the pure Mission style," having "a fine, distinctive, California flavor." Continuing with comments and illustrations of Mission Revival work by architects Parker, Stone, and Smith, the state-sponsored book contrasted the one-story, well-lighted and adequately ventilated mission-style school with the older, multi-story institutions. In another section the Department emphasized that the Mission Revival was coming into more frequent use and represented progressive school design. A photograph comparing the "Old and New" types of school architecture made this point, although it undermined the assertion made earlier that multi-story facilities were of inferior design by illustrating precisely this kind of Mission Revival school. The Arts and Crafts Movement, active at this time, also adopted an ideological stance on education and mission architecture. Proponents linked a philosophy of practicality and manual training to modern mission-style schools.[23]

In 1915 *Architect and Engineer* reprinted "California's Architectural Contribution" from the *School Board Journal*. "The typical California 'mission' school house is nearly ideal for the climatic conditions of the state. The open cloisters afford shelter from the glare and heat of the summer, and protection against the rain and wind of the winter . . . they allow plenty of fresh air under all conditions. The one-story buildings afford a minimum expense for construction and maintenance, and a maximum of safety against fire, panics and other dangers found in the compactly built school houses of the eastern states. Except for the greater ground area which they occupy—an objection that has no weight except in large cities—the mission type school has hardly a fault worth mentioning." After this time, public-school design shifted away from the Mission Revival, yet subsequent design incorporated the lessons of the style. The one-story format with outdoor corridors evolved into well-spaced wings of classrooms with surrounding playgrounds and sports fields. *Architectural Forum* remarked in 1917 that

California had come naturally by her "broad-spreading type of architecture in her school-houses," acknowledging again that a mission style was not the essential heritage, but rather that it was through principles of design derived from the Mission Revival that a really new type of school architecture had been brought about.[24]

As had been the case with residences, railway depots, and hotels, schools were also well-suited as promotional vehicles. "California has many . . . school buildings . . . None seem to be more in harmony with the surroundings and the history of the State than those erected along the lines of the old missions."[25] Boosterism was never far from the minds of collective school boards and chambers of commerce. There existed a tenacious belief that California's cultural growth depended upon its educational facilities, a belief reflected by the intensity of interest in the Mission Revival. Promotionalism, however, quickly descended to lesser levels. Cement, tile, and school-supply companies came to realize that the mission-style school was perfectly suited for advertisement campaigns. In particular, William H. Weeks's designs appeared repeatedly in the industrial ads for *Architect and Engineer*.

Today one sees only the remnants of what at one time must have been a surprisingly dominant mission-style urban fabric. Architects resorted to all media—wood, brick, stucco-frame, and concrete—for a Mission Revival extravaganza. Sometimes architects gave a full mission treatment to the building type, employing tile roof, arcade, tower, quatrefoil window, and gable. In other instances, a single feature might label the structure as mission. California's growth in the early twentieth century—combined with intense promotionalism—encouraged organizations, businesses, and philanthropic groups to commission buildings. Whereas mission-style schools served as community monuments, multi-purpose structures symbolized the popular—albeit diluted— image of a town might wish to secure. Overzealous patrons and builder-architects carried missionizing to an extreme. Finally, professionals and public alike would grow tired of the revival.

In the early years structures functionally closest to the historic missions dominated the scene. Not surprisingly, architects often designed churches in the Mission Revival. Religious affiliation apparently did not hinder widespread use of a style derived from the Catholic Church. In 1902 the Baptist Church of Long Beach commissioned a Mission Revival building from Henry F. Starbuck. Even before construction, Long Beach promotional literature cited and illustrated the church.[26] (Fig. 137) Other mission-style churches for all denominations were erected throughout the state. (Fig. 138-140) By 1925 a Mission Revival church could be found in nearly every community, large or small, in California—and often in towns in Wash-

137

138

139

137 Henry F. Starbuck, First Baptist Church, Long Beach, 1902. Perspective published in First Baptist Church, *Picturesque Long Beach*, 1902. (The Bancroft Library) [Demolished]

138 William H. Weeks, First Christian Church, Winters, 1912. (J. W. Snyder: 1979) [Now the Church of Jesus Christ of Latter Day Saints]

139 Edwards and Shoemaker, First Baptist Church, Fort Bragg, 1913. (J. W. Snyder: 1981)

Designed over a decade, the three churches really varied little. Protestant denominations commissioned each, and while their locations ranged from the extreme southern part of the state to the extreme north, they all looked incredibly alike. Prominent gables on two facades, with corner entry tower, accented a basically square structure. Fenestration, too, was strikingly similar. Of the three churches, that in Winters was the most impressive. And so it should have been: it was designed by William H. Weeks, an architect who had established a successful practice statewide by 1912.

140

140 John J. Foley, Saint Stanislaus Church, Modesto, 1914. (J. W. Snyder: 1980)

Catholic churches adhered to a more formal Mission Revival facade. Usually two-towered with quatrefoil rose window, the Catholic churches followed not only centuries-old traditions, but also the pattern of the California Franciscan mission church itself. Although the extended arcades present at the missions were not repeated in the revival designs, this too was appropriate, for the church did not often have a similar self-contained community life. San Francisco architect John J. Foley, the designer of St. Stanislaus, was commissioned for more than 100 Catholic churches and related buildings during his career.

141 Lester S. Moore, ''Design for County Courthouse,'' *Craftsman*, February 1904.

Lester S. Moore had been one of the prominent Mission Revival architects in Los Angeles during the late 1890s, working in partnership with J. J. Blick. By 1904 Moore's career had slowed—yet he still was designing in a mission style. Presented in *Craftsman*, his proposal for a Mission Revival courthouse never saw execution. In fact, very few courthouses were ever built in the style. For a community image less pretentious civic structures were chosen for a mission portrayal.

141

ington, Oregon, Nevada, Colorado, Arizona, New Mexico, and Texas. Hospitals, almshouses, funeral homes, sanatoriums, and orphanages also peppered cities with the Mission Revival from 1900 through 1925.

Other types susceptible to the Mission Revival were chamber of commerce facilities, city gateways, and clubhouses. (Fig. 141) Here promotionalism came to the fore, attracting tourists and generally advertising the town. Some visitors returned as residents. By 1906 B. G. McDougall had designed the chamber of commerce building for Fresno and the Hyde business block for Visalia. (Fig. 142) During the same period Santa Barbara received a proposal for a mission-style arch over downtown State Street. Stockton architect E. B. Brown also designed a welcoming arch for Lodi, a small San Joaquin Valley town. (Fig. 143) Masonic halls were yet another popular beneficiary of the Mission Revival. Santa Rosa and Yuba City were among the many cities that commissioned mission-style halls. (Fig. 144) In

142

143

142 B. G. McDougall, Hyde Business Block, Visalia, c. 1903-06. Published in *Architect and Engineer*, June 1906. [Demolished]

143 E. B. Brown, Arch, Lodi, 1907. (K. J. Weitze: 1980)

The highly visible business block was a perfect candidate for the revival. Benjamin G. McDougall, the middle son of Barnett McDougall, established a practice in the southern portion of the San Joaquin Valley. He designed numerous Mission Revival structures for Bakersfield, Fresno, Visalia, Porterville, and other nearby towns. His civic imagery was particulary noteworthy. At a more northerly location in the valley, Stockton architect E. B. Brown designed a mission-style welcome arch for Lodi. The arch was one of the best known community heralds ever translated into the idiom of the revival.

144 L. M. Turton, Masonic Hall, Yuba City, c. 1910. Perspective published in *Architect and Engineer*, October 1910.

Another source of community imagery was that presented by a town's fraternal halls and civic clubhouses. Many of these buildings were designed in a Mission Revival style during the first two decades of the twentieth century. Turton's Masonic Hall for Yuba City was typical.

144

1905 the California Club sponsored San Francisco's first women's building in the Mission Revival. And in 1909 *Architect and Engineer* published a notice entitled "Mission Architecture for Federal Buildings": "Supervising Architect James Knox Taylor announces that the Spanish or Mission style of architecture, with its belfry towers, red tiles, patios and arcades, shall be adopted for the buildings to be erected for the Government at San Diego, Santa Barbara, Riverside and, in fact, wherever Southern California public buildings shall be erected."[27]

Although other cities carried out similar policies, a singular irony remained: the state never commissioned a Mission Revival office building for the Sacramento bureaucracy. The Capitol building of 1860-74, in conjunction with offices erected on the grounds during the early 1880s, housed the state until the 1923-24 construction of the Court and Library Building and Office Building One. Thus, the revival waxed and waned entirely within a period of governmental containment, never once highlighting an official state facade outside those of exposition pavilions. Mission Revival remained first and foremost a colloquial idiom. Architects designed libraries, telephone offices, amusement pavilions, bookstores, post offices, banks, newspaper offices, opera houses, garages, and restaurants.[28] (Fig. 145-149) More unusual designs included freestanding bell towers, Charles Fletcher Lummis's Southwest Museum, Italian-Swiss Colony's concrete champagne building, and bridges in Oakland and Riverside.[29] (Fig. 150-152) Outside the state Mission Revival restaurants, a chocolate factory, and a stock pavilion mark several of the atypical published

145

146

147

145 Stone and Smith, Carnegie Library, Hayward, 1905. Published in *Architect and Engineer*, December 1908. [Demolished]

Libraries were also popular for a mission-style presentation. Architects applied revival details in widely different ways, yet the vocabulary was ever the same. Carnegie libraries, in particular, saw repeated Mission Revival treatment.

146 Plumas County Bank, Quincy, 1903. (J. W. Snyder: 1980)

147 Julia Morgan, Examiner Building, Los Angeles, 1912. (K. J. Weitze: 1978)

148 Charles and William Beasley, Engine House No. 3, Stockton, 1906-08. (K.J. Weitze: 1979)

149 Arthur B. Benton, Glenwood Garage [Mission Inn], Riverside, c. 1905-10. California Wheelmen, Good Roads Tour, 1912. (California Department of Transportation)

Mission Revival appeared in the full spectrum of building types, in all parts of California (and the West generally), and at every professional level. In some instances—like those exemplified by the Plumas County Bank—no architect was involved; rather it was a builder-contractor commission. Yet in other cases, a city's best-known architect (like Stockton's Beasleys) might easily have been behind a design. Even architects of regional and national reputation (like Julia Morgan) designed in a mission style. For public buildings, no pat formula ever evolved; the revival was continually varied. Only in the final years of the style's popularity did a vague pattern appear. By 1915-20, a simple, almost flattened, mission gable atop a building's facade might well be the only remaining reference to the revival.

149

150

151

150 John B. Leonard and Albert A. Farr, Oakland Avenue Bridge, Piedmont, 1911. Published in *Engineering News*, September 1911. [Modified]

Designed by civil engineer John B. Leonard and consulting architect Albert A. Farr, the Oakland Avenue Bridge in Piedmont was one of only a few Mission Revival bridges in California. Local real estate speculation undoubtedly had inspired the choice of style, with Piedmont civic officials seeking the fashionable Spanish imagery.

151 7th Street Bridge, Riverside, 1923. (Riverside Municipal Museum) [Replaced in 1958]

152 Widening of the 7th Street Bridge, 1930-31. (California Department of Transportation) [Replaced in 1958]

Designed very late in the span of years associated with the Mission Revival, the 7th Street Bridge in Riverside was a most remarkable structure. Ever since Frank Miller's first missionizing of the city (with the Mission Inn at the turn of the century), Riverside had witnessed the erection of numerous mission-style buildings. The revival tied the city together in thematic way, and, of course, it encouraged tourism. With its massive towers, the bridge was like nothing else in California. Even its electroliers and railing were executed as stylized mission bells. When the Division of Highways widened the bridge in 1930-31, it carefully moved and reincorporated the towers and other components to preserve the design. It was not until 1958 that the bridge was replaced altogether.

152

examples.[30] (Fig. 153) The vernacular appeal permeating
California Mission Revival occasionally filtered through more
established traditions in the East and Northeast, despite the
idiosyncratically Western argot of the style. Even Chinatown in
Victoria, British Columbia, sported a mission design in 1911.
(Fig. 154) Capturing the public imagination, the revival
touched many places.

153

153 Sidney B. Newsom, ''Eastern Chocolate Factory,''
Architect and Engineer, October 1912.

154 Lee's Benevolent Association, Chinatown, Victoria, British Columbia, 1911. (J. W. Snyder: 1981)
  Mission Revival buildings surfaced in unexpected
places. Sidney B. Newsom, son of Samuel, designed a
mission-style factory for the Miner Chocolate company
somewhere in the ''East.'' In Victoria, British Columbia,
a gabled, triple-arched Richardsonian Romanesque/
Mission Revival facade graced Lee's Benevolent Association in Chinatown. The revival had become so popular
that in instances like these it respected neither locale nor
ethnic idiosyncracies.

154

Chapter Five

Principles
for a New Era

*. . . it is rather by the lesson of quietness and moderation
they inculcate than by the technical "style" they offer
for direct imitation that the architectural labors
of the Franciscan missionaries have been most useful.*

Montgomery Schuyler, "Round About Los Angeles,"*Architectural Record,* December 1908

155

As early as the middle 1870s, two rationales for the Mission Revival, each intertwined with the other, began to take shape. Together they culminated in the advocacy of a mission style by the Arts and Crafts Movement and by the American cement industry. Arts and Crafts writers analyzed the missions as evocative of a tranquil, more meaningful existence. For many of them, Mission Revival possessed a simplicity that visually paralleled monastic life. Other commentators also linked the style with an austere aesthetic, tying it to innovations in the concrete industry. A Janus-faced movement of the late nineteenth and early twentieth centuries, the Mission Revival approached modernity through these associations. Unlike past revivals, it partook of Victorianism, yet clearly broke with Victorian traditions.

In 1875 Elizabeth Hughes wrote *The California of the Padres; or, Footprints of Ancient Communism,* in which she perceived the missions as idyllic, prototypical communes. A precursor to later Arts and Crafts interpretations, her essay focused sharply: "Homely and simple details . . . [the mission] was a sort of devotional industrial school, in which the Fathers were head laborers, head cooks, physicians and priests." Hughes contrasted mission life with the aggressive past of urban America. "The slow, tranquil years drifted by in the sunny Missions . . . while in the East . . . a great empire was being born . . . while the Padres were doing their work . . . Washington, Jefferson, Paine, and their illustrious compeers, were building . . . with sword and pen."[1] Progress equaled tumult and sometimes war, yet a peaceful brotherhood of humanity had a model in California. These sentiments surfaced again in the 1890s, when writers, artists, and architects joined the American Arts and Crafts Movement, espousing the tenets of British Socialist designer William Morris and searching for a solution to the complexity and alienation that was increasingly a part of the modern scene at the turn of the century. The same confusion that troubled Henry Adams, that motivated writers Theodore Dreiser and Edith Wharton, prompted an Arts and Crafts identification with the Mission Revival.

Concurrent with *American Architect and Building News's* reception of the Mission Revival in Southern California, *House*

155 "A Craftsman House," published in G. Stickley, *Craftsman Homes,* New York, 1909.
The mission-style Craftsman house of 1904 (published here in 1909) was straightforward in its simplicity. No ornamentation of any kind accented the residence—no gables, no quatrefoils, no towers. Only the practical veranda with its arched openings referenced the revival. For the Arts and Crafts, it was a matter of style appropriate to climate and geography.

Beautiful recognized the style, discussing it in an Arts and Crafts context. Predisposed toward articles on the builder-craftsman, the journal published Caroline L. Overman's "Modern Spanish Architecture in California" in December 1898. Observing that conventional American architectural models were not appropriate for California's climate, Overman mentioned the progressive work done in a Spanish style on Orange Grove Avenue in Pasadena. She further noted A. Page Brown's row houses in Santa Barbara as illustrative of the trend toward an architecture suited to its environment. The article concluded by remarking that Brown's houses—located in a residential area near Mission Santa Barbara—were "an adequate mental preparation for the best of the old Spanish churches."[2]

Charles Augustus and Louisa Keeler, too, were members of the coterie of California Arts and Crafts writers fascinated with the missions and the Mission Revival. The Keelers believed that the missions symbolized principles "of absolute sincerity, of immediate contact with nature, of loving interest in the work." Adhering to the philosophies of Britishers Pugin, Ruskin, and Morris, they continued, "The [missions] are literally hewn out of the surrounding land by the pious zeal of their makers. There is a softness and harmony about the lines which shows the work of hands instead of machines, and the dull red tiles and soft terra cotta and buff walls of stone are beautifully harmonious in color . . . the whitewashed walls of plaster are effective with the long, cool shadows of the arches." The missions epitomized a bygone era, an era prior to the industrial revolution. Charles Augustus Keeler commented, "I seemed transported into another land and another century, and a feeling of awe and wonder took possession of me."[3] Associating these sentiments with a revival of the mission form was the next step.

Immediately after the turn of the century two Arts and Crafts journals, *House Beautiful* and *Craftsmen*, addressed the Mission Revival directly. In a 1900 article on the patio, Olive Percival wrote for *House Beautiful* about the practical and romantic qualities of the courtyard. Several years later Hazel Waterman described the revival itself: "The simple dignity of the old mission designs is prevalent, and many of their characteristic features have been borrowed . . . the charm of the early hacienda life is intimately associated with it." In February 1902 *Craftsman* featured an essay on the Franciscans, demonstrating an even more intense focus than had *House Beautiful*. Like Elizabeth Hughes, the author contrasted the differing histories of the Western and Eastern United States. "What would have been the result if the Franciscans of Spanish California and the Puritans of Plymouth Rock had exchanged continent-sides on coming to America? For one thing we should have missed the most superb and harmonious type of architecture known to the new continent—the architecture of the Old Missions . . .

through all the troublous times of the American and French Revolutions, there on the halcyon western shore, the Franciscans were building and dwelling in pastoral peace and simplicity."[4]

In this same article *Craftsman* summarized the Arts and Crafts philosophies represented in the missions: communal property, manual and mental labor, an apprentice-like partnership between the skilled and unskilled, and a cooperative work spirit. More noteworthy, however, was the link established between the missions and the Mission Revival. "But the mission architecture is not entirely lost, for it is springing up into fresh life in some of the newer artistic structures of the West." Continuing, the author pointed to the campus design of Stanford University of the late 1880s and to the Californa Building of 1893 as the beginnings of the revival. To followers of the Arts and Crafts, Stanford's "home-like buildings" were especially attractive. For those initially involved with the movement, then, it was not the visual similarity between the historic missions and the revival that was significant, but rather that the revival evoked the "patient handicraft" and "loving sincerity" of the "unskilled builders who had joy and faith in their work."[5]

A growing awareness of the West as a unique region, distinct from other sections of the country, was yet another factor aligning the Arts and Crafts with the Mission Revival. Many individuals interpreted mission-style buildings, particularly residences, as suitable to the geography and climate. The low, outspread architecture, with its indoor-outdoor functionalism, bespoke the desire to treat a building in context. "Style . . . is not necessarily chosen from the accepted classic and Renaissance periods . . . style . . . is a frank expression of locality and the material at hand. In this *Craftsman* article of 1903, Franklin J. Hunt associated style with region. "Style would then really be synonymous with locality, and the locality of a country house would be an expression of local traditions, local necessities, limitations and possibilities of climate and landscape."[6]

As the twentieth century unfolded, an Arts and Crafts discussion became ever more progressive. In another *Craftsman* article of 1903, Harvey Ellis emphasized the lessons of honesty and simplicity, rather than those of imitation. With insight, Ellis coupled the work of early Mission Revivalists with that of Louis Sullivan, an architect whom he felt was "one of the few men in the United States . . . who have comprehended the meaning of the word architecture . . . who have forgotten the schools and become architects of equal ability with the good Franciscan Father Junipero Serra, the moving spirit in the designing and construction of the missions." In his later writings Charles Augustus Keeler, too, focused upon innovation. Keeler defined the modern, utilitarian residence in *The Simple Home* of 1904. Returning again to the principles underlying a mission style, he distinguished between sham revival and regional architecture. Keeler felt that the Mission Revival was not appropriate for Northern California's often more cloudy and damp climate, while for the southern part of the state mission design deserved attention. He concentrated on an architecture of integrity. "There is a romantic charm about such architecture and an historic association which California needs to cherish, but to mimic it with cheap imitations in wood is unworthy of us. If we are unwilling to take the pains, or if we cannot afford to do the work genuinely, let us not attempt it."[7]

In 1909 Gustav Stickley published *Craftsman Homes,* wherein he presented workshop designs that had been illustrated in *Craftsman* during the preceding five years. Although the California Arts and Crafts had shifted towards an architecture of wood-craftsmanship, Stickley referred to the contributions of the Mission Revival. The first house selected (from January 1904) was mission, recommended by *Craftsman* "in the belief that its simplicity, its vigorous style, and its picturesque quality, will find immediate favor." (Fig. 155) Two other Mission Revival residences, one of 1906 and another of 1909, were also included.[8] At this time San Diego architect Irving Gill also reflected Stickley's sentiments. "The Missions of California are beautiful because their builders could not but be honest. They had not the time, tools or skill to cover with ornament or cut-up into angle, so their works stand with undisputed dignity and superiority among the ornate, bizarre structures that now companion them . . . their [the missions'] extreme simplicity holds the eye, resting and gratifying it, making an indelible impression of power and repose."[9]

Regionalism, environmentalism, integrity, harmony, simplicity, sincerity—the Arts and Crafts linked each with the Mission Revival. Yet it was another issue—materials—that led the debate. Arts and Crafts writers accentuated the individual and the handmade, but were simultaneously fascinated with the technology of the concrete industry. Quickly, they associated concrete and stucco with handmade adobe. "The Californian country-house should be a one-story building, and to be still further consistent, tile and clay, or cement [concrete or stucco], which has replaced clay, should be used as materials." Stickley, too, noted concrete as important for residential architecture. Left unfinished, it gave the impression of a primitive building substance. In addition, Stickley felt that the neutral tone of concrete harmonized well with the light and color of its surroundings.[10]

Stucco and concrete were provocative materials for the early twentieth century.[11] For the Mission Revival, writers and architects asserted that these materials, like adobe, were proper for an architecture of simple proportions and molded form. The analogy, however, proved superficial. Adobe brick walls laid in

116

a masonry technique and coated with a white-washed plaster were fundamentally different from those of modern construction. The hardened mud and straw bricks revealed an architecture of individual units. By contrast, builders applied stucco, a calcined mixture of clay, lime, sand, and water, to a metal lath frame; and they poured concrete, a similar mixture combined with an aggregate, into a mold. Aesthetically, too, the effects of stucco and concrete only cursorily resembled those of adobe. Mission walls were three to six feet thick, while the depth of a molded concrete wall was much less. Ephemeral in nature, stucco on metal lath cracked and flaked over time. If anything, stucco allowed decorative play not found in the missions, whereas poured concrete offered a fluid uniformity.

Yet Arts and Crafts architects were not the first to compare adobe and concrete. Mistake or no, it was an analogy that had begun in the 1890s, and one which led through the Mission Revival toward modernity. In 1891 *California Architect and Building News* mentioned that repairs at Mission San Carlos at Carmel had been done with "cement stucco," thus implying a similarity, in effect and texture, between adobe and cement. During the 1891-92 debates surrounding the California Building, consideration of stucco on metal lath preoccupied architects' concern for the correct building material. By March 1893 argument even appeared in *Cosmopolitan*. Ellen Henrotin discussed the broad, flat wall surfaces and elementary forms of Spanish-American architecture as appropriate for stucco. "The stuff used in the construction of the buildings of the Columbian exposition is like the adobe of which Mexican houses are built, and in the future this material [stucco] is destined to be largely employed in America."[12]

P. B. Wright, too, acknowledged the structural consequence of the California Building in his review of the exposition for *American Architect and Building News*. "The largest number of the buildings are frame covered with staff [a type of stucco used for temporary construction] and plaster . . . Of this class are the New York State Building and the California State Building, which are architecturally and structurally the best in the northern section." Wright continued, stating that the California Building was "a correct illustration of early Hispano-American architecture . . . the first coat of plaster on it is cement, it can easily be kept in repair." Here again was the presumption that construction techniques in the coming century might well accommodate a revival of California's historic architecture.[13]

Perhaps most noteworthy of all, critic Montgomery Schuyler singled out the California Building in an article for *Architectural Record*. His points were dynamic, providing sound formalistic reasoning for a mission style. "It happens that the modifications made by the missionaries in the architecture they tried to naturalize are such as to fit it especially for reproduction at the

World's Fair. The adobe that they were forced to substitute for masonry has much the same characteristics and possibilities as the 'staff,' or tough plaster which is the envelope of the buildings at Jackson Park." Although he, too, employed the analogy with adobe, Schuyler recognized the roles played by shadow and light, solid and void, smoothness and texture in an adaptation of stucco techniques to the Mission Revival. "The shadows of the eaves . . . give strong and emphatic belts that accentuate a division in itself carefully studied and effective, while the corrugation of the tiles . . . gives character to the roofs themselves, and an effective contrast to the smooth walls which is very gently heightened by the contrast in color of the gray plaster and the deep red tiles." Commenting further, the critic observed that while the walls remained simple, planar surfaces, plaster gave them an appearance of depth and massiveness. Concluding, he praised the California Building as "one of the most attractive and appropriate of all the buildings at Jackson Park."[14]

Sporadically during the first years of the Mission Revival, 1895-99, articles and pamphlets amplified the analysis. Charles Fletcher Lummis remarked in his 1895 essay, "The Lesson of Adobe," that stucco on metal lath and "solid cement" [concrete] could be adapted to simulate the smooth surfaces of adobe. At the close of the decade the cement industry itself issued booklets that made similar assertions. The California Portland Cement Company noted that concrete buildings were less time consuming to erect and less costly than the standard masonry structure. In addition, the industry made a case for the strength and durability of the new material. In an 1899 handbook the company clinched the argument for a stucco-on-concrete construction by concluding that the technique had "the advantage of the Mexican adobe." Tile manufacturers, too, soon realized the potential business represented by the Mission Revival. In 1898 the Cleveland Hydraulic-Press Brick Company published *Early Religious Architecture*, a book chiefly composed of California and Southwestern mission photographs. A brief introduction stated that the missions were "by a strictly material standard . . . worthy of the closest study," having "elements of the highest value." They were "artistically perfect." The industry itself could gladly manufacture mission tile, indicating a shrewd awareness of what the style might mean for company growth.[15]

Although the transitions of the 1890s were significant, it was the year 1904 that marked a turning point. Cement manufacturers had commented upon the absence of a U.S. pavilion at the 1893 Columbian Exposition, noting that it was a glaring omission when juxtaposed to the exhibit hosted by the German industry. To rectify their competitive image, the Association of American Portland Cement Manufacturers decided to sponsor an elaborate pavilion at the Louisiana Purchase Exposition in St. Louis. They chose a Mission Revival design as representative of the industry. (Fig. 156) "The exhibit building . . . is an excellent example of reinforced concrete construction, and consists of three pavilions separated by intermediate courts and connected across the front by a continuous loggia, the roof of which is covered with cement tiling (Spanish pattern) of a rich red color."[16]

Texture and color were uppermost in the minds of the association's architects: "the red tinting of the ceiling of the loggia, relieve[s] the general grey tone of the walls and forms an agreeable color contrast . . . the rough-finished walls are particularly well adapted to the use of concrete." To make certain that no mistake occurred in the labeling of the buildings, the official 1904 pamphlet designated the style as "Spanish Mission." In an exposition in which the pavilions were designed in a "free renaissance style," both the California Building and that of the Portland cement manufacturers were Mission Revival. California's rationale was self-explanatory, but classical design was a viable choice for the cement industry. The Portland Cement Association, however, did not consider that stylistic treatment to be expressive of a progressive image.[17]

Architects focused upon issues of style and materials most actively from 1905 through 1910. *Architect and Engineer* featured articles on concrete, cement, and tile; while *Cement Age*, too, chaired discussion and argument. In June 1905 *Cement Age* analyzed a Jamaican concrete residence, emphasizing its appropriateness for the island. "A tropical climate with its attending

156 Portland Cement Association, pavilion, Louisiana Purchase Exposition, St. Louis, 1904. Published in Portland Cement Association, *Bulletin*, St. Louis, 1904.

The Portland Cement Association's pavilion for the Louisiana Purchase Exposition in St. Louis of 1904 was the second most telling building of its kind. California's state pavilion at the Columbian Exposition in Chicago of 1893 had been the first—it had announced the Mission Revival. But what the cement industry's pavilion accomplished was equally significant, even if more subtle. A Mission Revival pavilion representative of the American industry let it be known that during the first years of the twentieth century one of the cutting edges for concrete design was to be a mission style.

156

moisture, profuse and luxurious plant life and endless varieties of destructive insects, at once suggests the advantages, and almost the necessity, of masonry construction from the standpoint of sanitation, material comfort, and durability." *Architectural Record* of 1905 also carried an article on all-concrete villas. Essays suggesting that tile roofs, modeled after those of Spanish type, were an accompaniment to the concrete structure appeared as well.[18]

Bringing these issues into perspective, architect William L. Price of Philadelphia lectured to the Association of Portland Cement Manufacturers in 1906. Stressing the abandonment of traditional American styles, the speaker called for innovation. "But in a material so plastic the forms of openings and mouldings may be expected to vary much from those necessary to an architecture dependent on arches and lintels. There is more to be learned in the Spanish, or Californian and Mexican varieties of Spanish, than any other accepted type." Unlike other analysts, Price concentrated on the illusion of plasticity present in the adobe missions, while simultaneously acknowledging its unit composition. "Their plastered walls, tile roofs and wall copings suggest concrete more than they do brick, and their domes and curved pediments are already suggestive of plastic rather than block construction." The same year *American Builders Review* put it even more bluntly: "it is the increasing use of plaster and cement as a surfacing material in America that has called the attention of our designers to these mission buildings in the far West."[19]

After 1906 assessments of Mission Revival's application to modern concrete architecture became a pronounced topic in both professional journals and industry pamphlets.[20] In 1907 architectural and engineering periodicals published more essays arguing the artistic possibilities of concrete than in any other single year. In April David Lay, writing for *Cement Age*, began the debate: "Lack of beauty is the cry against concrete houses to-day. Whatever truth there is in such accusation is the fault rather of the users than the materials." Insisting that the material could be treated tastefully, Lay announced that concrete had come to stay. Again the California missions were advocated as a model. "It [concrete] requires then a concrete architecture characteristically its own. It needs an art of concrete . . . The nature of concrete leads to its use in large flat wall spaces. That such may be treated artistically has been proved by the stucco work in . . . the missions of Mexico and California." He concluded, however, by asking that architects not copy the missions—but that they learn from them, remembering that concrete was a more refined material than adobe.[21]

Architect A. O. Elzner continued the 1907 discussion in papers read before the National Association of Cement Users and the American Institute of Architects in May and November. Citing the Pacific Coast's historic example, he noted, "Perhaps the best sources of inspiration that can be had for such treatment are to be found in the old Spanish missions of California, which, although not of concrete, nevertheless at once suggest its use and above all are fine examples of the artistic value of broad wall-surfaces relieved by exquisitely proportioned openings judiciously spaced." Elzner further recommended that the imprint of form-boards be left unfinished, extrapolating that the Padres would have done the same had their material been concrete. In November, the architect reiterated the value of the mission model. It "avoided the eccentricities and pitfalls of L'Art Modern, or Neauveau [*sic*] art. Such is the spirit which should possess and guide the designer of concrete today."[22]

Yet another architect, A. D. F. Hamlin, addressed the issues for *American Architect and Building News,* commenting that "the so-called 'mission architecture' of the Southwest offers suggestions which should be useful to the designer of a monolithic building." Hamlin, like Lay before him, was aware that the Mission Revival offered only a partial solution. "It is evident that in large and complex buildings there must be many experiments and much invention and adaptation before satisfactory results will be secured."[23] Both men had touched upon an issue that would soon achieve eminence. Artistic principles of simplicity and proportion appropriate for a plastic, monolithic architecture were those that merited architects' attention. Imitating a past building type, in this instance through the Mission Revival, was no more than a stepping stone to design without reliance on revivalism.

During this ideologically stormy year Irving K. Pond also cited the California missions as a provocative model for concrete design. In the 1880s, the architect had heralded Spanish architecture as an exemplar for the modern period. By 1907 he had narrowed his focus: "The Spanish missions were built with rare feeling for mass and light and shade; but feeling swayed and science did not guide. With the science of today to guide and the art experience of the past to illumine, into what logical, noble and beautiful forms should not concrete shape itself, to the end of an enduring, spiritualized architecture." Pond implored his fellows to abandon "piling up child's building blocks on a large scale" and to work towards "a molded architecture . . . an architecture of flowing and harmoniously inter-related masses."[24]

In 1907 *House and Garden* published "The Use of Portland Cement for Modern Dwellings," an article which further illuminated the debated issues. Writer Seymour Coates praised "cement plaster" as a twentieth century product that allowed "restraint and freedom from ornamentation." Most informative, however, were the illustrations. Seven Mission Revival residences in the Los Angeles area were selected to demonstrate the architectural possibilities of stucco on metal lath. Undoubtedly, the intention was to choose those houses that represented the spectrum of excellence projected for the style. The residences included those of W.C. Stuart (1895), Jas. H. Adams (c. 1894-97), D.M. Smyth (1897), and Frank W. Emery (1897), as well as three houses of more recent date. (fig. 157-158) A magazine with an Arts and Crafts orientation, *House and Garden* was soon followed by *Craftsman*. Una Nixon Hopkins emphasized that "plaster" architecture was most effective in the West and Southwest. Here the legitimacy sought in Arts and Crafts architecture was perceived as derived from the practical use of concrete or stucco construction. "Cement . . . is the material par excellence for a dulcet, semitropical climate such as lower California, where it does not suffer from the ravages of atmosphere, merely mellows and grows old beautifully."[25]

157

158

157 L. L. Bourgeois, M. Paul DeLongpre House, Hollywood, c. 1900-01. Published in *House and Garden*, September 1907.

French painter M. Paul DeLongpre arrived in Los Angeles in 1899, settling in Hollywood. His Mission Revival estate was then the height of fashion, while the extensive floral gardens complemented not only the residence itself, but also the artist's career.

158 Hunt and Eager, Beville House, Hollywood, c.1905. Published in *House and Garden*, September 1907.

Hunt and Eager's Beville House, like that of Paul DeLongpre, was one of a growing number of Mission Revival residences in Hollywood. During the 1900-11 years, the style achieved its height of popularity.

159 Julia Morgan, Mills College Campanile, Oakland, 1904. Published in *Architect and Engineer*, April 1908.

Julia Morgan's Mission Revival campanile for Mills College was just one of many reinforced concrete structures featured in the pages of *Architect and Engineer* as representative of the "artistic possibilities" accompanying innovative technology. The revival really served as a transition towards a greater understanding of the concrete medium.

Articles noting the relevance of Mission Revival design for reinforced concrete were soon to follow. In 1908 Charles F. Whittlesey pronounced the advantages of the medium for *Architect and Engineer*, illustrating his text with several mission-style buildings. A. O. Elzner again wrote on the artistic treatment of concrete, restating his praise for the missions. The California professional journal also referred to Ernest Ransome's patent for reinforced concrete and its use by architect Julia Morgan in a Mission Revival campanile for Mills College. (Fig. 159) At the close of the year, critic Montgomery Schuyler analyzed the range of questions that had surfaced in 1907 and 1908, climaxing arguments of the preceding months. Writing for *Architectural Record*, he remarked, "It is evident how well the style, the style of the Missions, lends itself to the construction in concrete which so many are prone to believe is the coming method of building." Keenly striking on the point that so many had been unable to articulate, Schuyler cut through to the heart of the debates: "But it is rather by the lesson of quietness and moderation they inculcate than by the technical 'style' they offer for direct imitation that the architectural labors of the Franciscan missionaries have been most useful." Later, in 1910, *Cement Age* called for a "distinct and original style" for concrete, noting that the development might answer "the problem of the fugitive '20th century style'."[26]

During these years *Cement Age* featured California buildings.[27] In an article of 1908, the journal illustrated a concrete bungalow, commenting that the "early Latin type" residence was "one of the notable examples of concrete houses now becoming quite numerous in southern California." *Cement Age* examined several additional buildings in 1910, including a Mission Revival wine plant, a San Jose school, and a Sacramento hotel. Speaking of the school, the journal characterized it as unequaled from an aesthetic standpoint. "It stands as one of California's latest and most satisfactory examples of artistic reinforced concrete construction." In 1909 Octavius Morgan, a Los Angeles architect writing for *Architect and Engineer*, summarized many opinions in a tribute to concrete: "We in Los Angeles and in Southern California, have some of the best examples of plastic cement work in the country, yes, in the world. What has been accomplished is merely suggestive of what can and will be accomplished in the future with cement."[28]

The intensity associated with the 1907-10 professional debates also carried over into the private promotional arena of the Portland cement manufacturers. Showcasing mission-style mansions in the Northeast, the Atlas Portland Cement Company printed *Concrete Country Residences* in 1907. Here not only were gables, towers, and quatrefoils abused, but they were also misadapted for New England. The Ernest Queen House in Glen Cove, Long Island, a stucco-on-brick residence designed

159

by C. P. H. Gilbert, combined Federal and Mission Revivals in an unlikely rendition that included an elaborate stable. (Fig. 160-161) In neighboring Bristol, Rhode Island, Carl P. Johnson, collaborating with Parkhurst and Kissam, designed a reinforced-concrete residence with boathouse for W. H. Knight. (Fig. 162-163) Other examples filled the volume, demonstrating how the industry had taken a Western style and made it palatible for the Atlantic Coast. (Fig. 164) From formal

160

161

160-161 C. P. H. Gilbert, Ernest Queen House and Stable, Glen Cove, Long Island, c. 1907. Published in Atlas Portland Cement Company, *Concrete Country Residences*, New York, 1907.

Not surprisingly, it was in New England that the Mission Revival was most out of touch with the Southwestern regionalism that had spawned the style. A "mission" mansion with Federal details, like the two story columns and pilasters of the Ernest Queen House, seems impossible. Yet it existed, as did its Mission Revival stable.

162

163

162-163 Carl P. Johnson, in collaboration with Park-
hurst and Kissam, W. H. Knight House and Boathouse,
Bristol, Rhode Island, c. 1907. Published in *Concrete
Country Residences.*

By its very existence, the W. H. Knight residence
gives pause for reflection. Two keen ironies of the Mission Revival are encapsulated in its design. First, such
mansions are proof of the revival's popularity—even
in unlikely places. It was fashionable: the wealthy of
New England commissioned architects to design in a
style that logically they should not have acknowledged. And second, the cement industry chose these
very inappropriate Mission Revival houses to prop-
agandize the relationship between concrete architecture and a historic mission model. They published
the mansions of New England, not those of Southern
California.

164 Clough and Wardner, E. Y. Bliss House, Boston,
c. 1907. Published in *Concrete Country Residences.*

Photographed in winter, the E. Y. Bliss House illustrated yet another incongruity for a Mission Revival on
the Atlantic seaboard: snow. No palm trees here. Yet
suitability to climate and geography was not the major
argument of the cement manufacturers. Instead it
remained always "form appropriate for concrete."

164

165

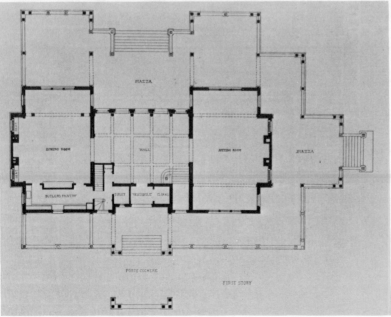

166

165-166 A. J. Manning, Alfred J. Nathan House, Elberon, New Jersey, c. 1905. Perspective and plan published in *American Homes and Gardens,* October 1905.

Occasionally, some of the broader lessons of the revival were not lost, even if transmuted to a different region. The airy grounds of the A. J. Nathan House tied it in spirit to a milder climate, although the functional shutters portrayed a more accurate reality.

167

167 Mission Revival house, in M. Sloan, *The Concrete House and Its Construction*, Philadelphia, 1912.

Illustrating a range of mission-style houses, from the extremely simple to the very ornate, Sloan's *Concrete House and Its Construction* exemplified the role of the revival in the pattern book industry. For the 1904-12 period, adaptation of mission details was interpreted as particularly appropriate for concrete design, and was so sanctioned and promoted by the cement manufacturers themselves.

rose gardens to functional shutters, inappropriate details mattered little.[29] (Fig. 165-166)

Builder manuals appeared in rapid succession in 1911 and 1912, with several featuring the revival and noting its relevance for concrete. Of some prominence were *Distinctive Homes of Moderate Cost, Successful Houses and How to Build Them*, and *The Concrete House and Its Construction*. In the latter the American Portland Cement Manufacturers treated the subject comprehensively. Author Maurice Sloan listed the effects of broad, simple wall surfaces, neutral coloration accented by touches of brightness, and massive form as best suited for concrete architecture. (Fig. 167) Closing his presentation, he wrote, "If there is one style of architecture with which monolithic concrete construction fits better than another, it is the California or Mexican 'Mission,' as expressed in the low rambling buildings with the deep recessed porches and Spanish tiled roofs so favorably known and extensively used in California."[30]

Manufacturers and builders, however, finally turned all efforts towards salesmanship. *Architect and Engineer* advertised "Acme Keene's Cement Mission Hardwall Plaster," and "Mission Cement Coating." The Atlas Portland Cement Company bolstered its ads with photographs of Mission Revival houses.[31] Mass-produced books on the concrete bungalow, available to anyone who cared to choose a design and submit a bid, provided further opportunity for the manipulation of a popular image. The result was literally thousands of mission-style buildings, many of which were individually poorly designed, and all of which—together—obliterated the distinctiveness of the early revival.[32]

The serious, however, continued to be intertwined with the superficial. At this time the Germans too were evaluating innovations made in the Portland cement industry. In 1910 Rudolf Vogel, in *Das Amerikanische Haus,* discussed the evolution of concrete design. Vogel stated, "the nature of the plaster construction encourages its own particular form." For substantiation, he referred readers to three provocative American houses—two of Frank Lloyd Wright's Chicago suburban residences and the 1901-02 Burrage House in Redlands, California. The latter was unequivocally Mission Revival. Vogel saw concrete domestic architecture as taking two differing casts, one a geometric, austere configuration of massed units as executed by Wright, and the other, an architecture of sculptural molding as executed by Charles Brigham.[33]

Like Vogel, most professionals concurred in the belief that an architectural revolution was taking place—promotionalism or no. Concrete and stucco overturned the preeminence of traditional materials in the minds of many designers. The simultaneous development of the Mission Revival and of the concrete industry was more than coincidental. For a brief period they were intimately bound. Yet revivalism belonged to the nineteenth century. Was it really valid for concrete design? Did it look towards the future? By 1912-15, many architects were openly expressing such doubts, calling for an "honesty of purpose" and asking that "concrete . . . stand for concrete." Architect Irving K. Pond reassessed his position in 1915. Still praising the missions, he indicated that they should be used only as a reference, not as a sanctioned prototype for imitation. Pond's sentiments became even more severe by 1920. "Because concrete has for so long been placed into moulds or forms and because of the coarseness of some of its ingredients . . . the earlier designers . . . being dependent upon precedent, and knowing not where else to look, fell upon the crude Spanish detail and broad masses of the early Spanish Missions as representative of what best might be embalmed in concrete. And so Spanish missions distorted into bungalows and cottages and palaces spread like a rash over the face of the country."[34]

In 1884 Pond had been among the first to assert a correlation between Spanish architecture and modern residential design, giving his avid support in 1907 to the application of concrete technology for a mission style. Yet by the second decade of the twentieth century, his frustration was that of many architects and designers. California businessmen, institutions, and manufacturers had abused the Mission Revival. Architects, including Pond, had lost sight of the fact that the initial employers of a mission style had attempted to evaluate questions of both historic and contemporary relevance. After the experimental period of 1900-10, architects moved beyond revivalism, retaining the principles gained from experience with it. Pond's plea for architects "to exploit nothing, but to develop the latent and inherent possibilities of a worthy material" shows how empty the Mission Revival had become for many, yet does not indicate how enlightening it had been during its earliest manifestations.[35]

Chapter Six

A Victorian Dilemma

*Thus has been awakened an interest in . . . the Spanish Missions . . .
presenting a peculiar base of American architecture . . .
adapted to the climate and environment . . . embodying certain
historic ideas . . . and suggestive of modern requirements.*

Arthur Howard Noll, "The Spanish Missions of the Pacific Coast,"
American Architect and Building News, June 5, 1897

168

In 1867 Samuel Sloan published *Homestead Architecture*, a book containing residential designs in "Grecian, Italian, Gothic" and "numerous well-known sub-styles." Writing about the question of style, the architect noted that "no design in this work can be pointed out as a fac-simile of any ancient or foreign specimen of architecture; but ancient forms and details have too long appealed to the tastes or prejudices of mankind for the architect to dream of their abandonment."[1] Betraying American architects' rationale for eclecticism during the nineteenth century, Sloan also intimated their dissatisfaction with the continued acceptance of revivals. By the 1880s such rumblings were beginning to be heard even in California, that outpost of architectural design farthest West from the centers of professional discussion.

California Architect and Building News commented as early as 1880 on the growing confusion. "This year it is the English Gothic, the next in the reign of Queen Anne, the year after the French Renaissance, or perhaps a mixture of every style, by way of being eccentric." Copyism was truly a Victorian dilemma—one which was the subject of much debate. The journal persisted: "We trust that the day is not far distant when a restraint will be put upon this wild license of practice, and that good judgment and taste will take the place of the medley of styles and meretricious ornamentation which offend the eye." In such statements lay the genesis of a philosophy that not only would seek a style to replace all previous ones, but also would incorporate simple and straightforward design. By December the same year the *News* carried its indictment another step forward, noting that California's relative isolation had encouraged architects to indulge their clients. "Time, however, will regulate these things; and in years to come these effervescent wishes of owners, and the faulty willingness of architects to encourage and work out any new suggestion presented, however ridiculous and inconsistent with well-understood properties and harmonies, will give place to greater uniformities and an appreciation of the more substantially beautiful in architecture."[2]

In late 1881 *California Architect and Building News* once more remarked that it deplored the hodge-podge, this time emphasizing not only that in California was something new

168 Spier and Rohns, Grand Trunk depot, Battle Creek, Michigan, c. 1906. Published in *Western Architect*, December 1906.
Spier and Rohns designed this rather fantastic Mission Revival depot for the Grand Trunk Railway. A subsidiary of the Canadian National, the Grand Trunk operated lines across the United States-Canadian border from Toronto to Chicago and from Windsor, Ontario, to Buffalo, as well as a line across the lower Michigan peninsula. The Battle Creek depot was on the Toronto-to-Chicago run. The harsh-wintered Michigan locale and Canadian ownership could hardly have been more removed from the origins of the revival.

desired for the architectural scene, but also that throughout the country there was a call for fresh thinking. By February 1882 the journal fused the Californian and American cries for innovation. "The time must come sooner or later (and why not now?), when an original *American style* must be born of the national genius." While debating the probable evolution of style both nationally and regionally, the *News* declared the next month, "The Eastlake is no longer popular (in the Eastern States). The so-called Queen Anne style is said to be dead and laid upon the shelf. What is to follow is a matter of some concern to those who cater to fashion." Prophetically analyzing the situation in California and, to some extent, in the entire country, the journal pointed the way towards an adoption of the Mission Revival. "The public is tired of the straight lines, the sharp angles, and the formal decorations derived from English models."[3] Although it was not known at the time of this article, a mission style—with its Spanish origins, sculptural mass, and simple ornamentation—would satisfy these requirements.

Susan Power, writing for *Overland Monthly* in 1883, was among the first to plead for a distinctive California architecture. Unlike others who cited only differences of climate, geography and tradition, Power referred directly to the Victorian dilemma: "It will be a happy day in this country when we begin to study design and decoration principally to find something suited to our time and needs, instead of laboriously trying to force the present into the garb of the past. It will not be long until the architect will cease to search portfolios in quest of Jacobite or Tudor mansion, which he can transfer bodily to the grounds of a Rhode Island cotton-spinner, or some absurd imitation of feudal halls for a tradesman who has made a good thing in mess pork."[4] In her assessment of the adobe as a model for California architecture, Power saw the development of regional design—based on traditional forms yet not mimicking them—as the road to modernity.

Many, however, saw the missions as America's only authentic ruins; thus it was only a short step to succumb to the romance of a revival. In an article for *Scribner's* in May 1889, Charles Eliot Norton lamented the lack of a more substantial heritage. "In our country, barren as it is of historic objects that appeal to the imagination and arouse the poetic associations that give depth and charm to life, such a home is even more precious than in lands where works abound that recall the past by transmitting its image to our eyes."[5] The Mission Revival answered this desire for an architecture evocative of America's history in a way that paralleled England's adoption of the Gothic Revival. Previously, all revivals had been imported. A mission style was indigenous.

Discussion became heated with competitions for the California Building. *Architectural Record* reported in mid-1891:

"With us, one of the most popular of modern architectural ideas is that there will some day be devised a truly original American style." Writer Barr Ferre noted that the question was really untenable, however. "Our land is of such extent, it covers so many degrees of latitude and longitude that it would be impossible to impress any one style of architecture upon it, except by law or the arbitrary caprice of fashion. An architecture which would be suited to the semitropical climate of Florida would be totally out of place in the cold bleak temperature of Maine. The salubrious climate of California requires a very different kind of dwelling from that adapted to the hot summers and cold winters of Pennsylvania and New York." Yet Ferre did observe that American *styles* of architecture, based on the qualities present in the separate regions of the country, would be a feasible approach to national design.[6] Perhaps this aspect of the protracted debates underscored Daniel Burnham's stipulation that the state buildings for the Columbian Exposition represent their regions, and that those of the West and Southwest be mission in type. It is also possible that such arguments influenced the California World's Fair Commission in their deliberations. Could a mission revival be the elusive answer to an American style?

The opening of the exposition spurred arguments forward. Commenting that a "new school of architecture is arising in this country," Ellen M. Henrotin stated that while the Beaux-Arts would initiate a vogue for a French mode of design, "the Spanish school" would have "great influence in forming the American." On both counts her forecasts were accurate. In 1897 *American Architect and Building News* summarized the effects of the California Building, again alluding to its significance for the development of an American style. "The California Building at the Columbian Exposition, in 1893, afforded an opportunity to examine a style of architecture that might be regarded as the Pacific Coast analogue of the old Colonial buildings of the Atlantic States. The same style was made a dominant architectural feature also of the California Midwinter Fair . . . Thus has been awakened an interest in what are known as the Spanish Missions of the Pacific Coast, as presenting a peculiar base of American architecture capable of furnishing a distinct style of design; already adapted to the climate and environment of the Pacific Coast; embodying certain historic ideas worthy of perpetuation, and suggestive of development to meet modern requirements."[7]

During the first years of the Mission Revival debate intensified. Writing for *Lippincott's* in January 1896, John Stewardson commented, "With this unparalleled amount of serious work in architecture no one can yet say what the outcome of it will be as to that much mooted question, the American style. Among architects, nothing is so much talked about, argued about, almost fought about. Nor does this field of discussion lie fallow among laymen. The people of this country never took so much intelligent interest in architecture as they do to-day." Stewardson described the period as a time unlike any that had gone before it, one which possessed infinite potential for style and design. Continuing, he noted that some had accused America of being "without traditions worthy of the name, without noble examples of native architecture to be inspired from."[8] Although Stewardson did not elaborate, it is apparent that discussions of the missions as a design model— discussions that extended from the late 1880s through the 1920s—focused on this very issue.

In 1901 the public and the architectural profession alike clearly equated an American style with the Mission Revival at the Pan-American Exposition in Buffalo. Frederick S. Lamb, writing for *Craftsman* in October 1902, remarked that among the lessons to be learned from the fair was one of style. "With a logical, comprehensive plan, with an American style architecture, the California Spanish Mission, the founders of the Exposition endeavored to obtain, and succeeded in obtaining, the most elaborate and artistic exterior sculpture, color and illumination, yet attempted."[9] Here too, architects associated a mission style with a national concept of design, but with greater emphasis, for both European and American professionals attended the exposition.

Arguments continued unabated during the year of the Louisiana Purchase Exposition in St. Louis. Charles Collins, writing for *American Architect and Building News*, observed with discouragement that the question of an American style remained unresolved. Instead, the United States had produced only provincial designs, ones derived from regional traditions and climate, exemplified in the state buildings erected for national expositions. Commenting that each region was creating a characteristic architecture, Collins made a special reference to the mission style. "In Florida and especially in California the Spanish element is strongly expressed in the Mission Architecture."[10] Tied to an American style more than any other local manifestation, the Mission Revival was the best articulated of the regional developments.

Yet, could a mission style—with its obvious bonds to the West and Southwest—really address larger issues? Could it become accepted coast to coast? Certainly the railroads employed the revival as if it were a national phenomenon. Bismarck, North Dakota, and Battle Creek, Michigan, each had their mission depot. (Fig. 168) In 1906 *American Builders Review* analyzed the matter once again. Enos Brown submitted that "the type of architecture . . . she [Spain] introduced four centuries ago . . . still remains . . . to be widely adopted and perhaps to be the foundation upon which our national type of architecture may be erected." In the same issue Frank Chouteau Brown affirmed this position. "The picturesque remains of these missions exist today, long after Spain, with her soldiers and missionaries, has been swept from this continent, with sufficient vitality of type and such apparent relevance to their *locale* that within the last few years they have become the proto-types for a new style of dwelling that bids fair to become so immensely popular as to overrun the country."[11]

That same year *Architectural Record* suggested that a Pueblo Revival might be the answer. "If it be true . . . that the characteristics of good architecture are that a building shall be in harmony with its surroundings; that the exterior shall be in right relation to the interior, the elevation being a natural development of the plan; and that it shall be free from meaningless and meretricious ornament, then Pueblo American Architecture is good architecture, and deserves a moment of consideration; and it further possesses the merit of being a frank and logical expression of its purpose, and of the materials used."[12] Appropriateness to the given conditions of a region, emphasis on simplicity in design and articulated expression of function and structure—all demonstrated that current issues were uppermost in the writer's thoughts. Again, the dilemma was truly Victorian. The rationale was still veiled in revivalism, Americanized by its ties to an indigenous architectural type. The Mission and Pueblo Revivals were perceived as similar due to their correlative use of concrete, stark formality, and historic appeal. Hence, they were candidates for an original, American style, while at the same time appearing analogous to the Greek and Gothic Revivals.

By 1908 and 1909 many architects concluded that an American style was not possible. Louis Mullgardt was of this opinion. "In view of the great length and breadth of our land it is a mooted question as to whether we will ever have a style of architecture which may be termed distinctly national. Our ambitions and customs in various parts of our country are sufficiently diverse, likewise our climate, to prevent anything which might possibly savor of uniformity." *Architect and Engineer* described the Mission Revival as a waning fad, noting that "the tendency today . . . is to revert to the Colonial style, the impression seeming to have spread that the Mission style is neither a permanent nor a true California style." Citing the concrete bungalow as the great bastardizer of the style, the journal observed that "Perhaps it is the abortions that have been called 'Mission,' perpetuated in the name of architecture and exhibited in too many cheap constructions, that have turned a great many prospective builders against this style."[13]

Others, too, had become dissatisfied with the indiscriminate character of the Mission Revival, remarking that, while it had acquired vernacular favor, it had lost those stylistic aspects worthy of studied attention. Garden Mitchell, commenting for *Architect and Engineer*, stated, "One thing one does not see in Mexico is a certain style of architecture which is known as the Spanish Mission style, in which about three feet of tile roof is stuck against the front wall of the building so that the enlightened may know that it is Spanish."[14] For those believing in copyism as appropriate for the twentieth century, such sentiments were ignored. Subsequently, yet another revival, the Spanish Colonial, came to replace the mission style. Those individuals favoring revivalism contended that it was more accurately based on historic precedent than the Mission Revival had ever been. And perhaps they were correct. Yet no intense debates surrounded the Spanish Colonial. It was more simply a revival that had pulled away from progressive trends.

Several architects came to terms with an American style by assessing revivals as a stepping stone to the future. Charles Peter Weeks wrote for *Architect and Engineer*, "It is the architect who studies old world architecture literally, instead of copying the spirit of his fellow pioneer that is clogging the wheels of progress towards a consistent, harmonious architecture for America, only differing in different localities due to changed local conditions." Thus, the Mission Revival was the starting point for one of California's finest architects: Irving Gill. Yet another architect, Cass Gilbert, accurately predicted that a distinctive American residential type would evolve out of the concrete bungalow, a type itself derived from the Mission Revival.[15]

Architects acknowledged those components of the revival that left their imprint on California's residences and schools—the patio and arcade—as the most worthwhile contributions of Western and Southwestern regionalism.[16] In 1916 Irving Gill captured this significance. "The Missions have taught us also the beauty and usefulness of the court. Ramona's house, a landmark as familiar in the South as some of the Missions, was built around three sides of an open space, the other side being a high garden wall. This home plan gave privacy, protection and beauty . . . the archway that runs along the three sides formed by the house made the open-air living rooms . . . There was always a sheltered and a sunny side, always seclusion and an outlook into the garden. In California we have liberally borrowed this home plan, for it is hard to devise a better, cozier, more convenient or practical scheme for a home. In the seclusion of the outdoor living rooms and in their nearness to the garden, the arrangement is ideal." Another author wrote in 1939, "out of the stately missions of the devoted Padres, the ancient farmhouses of the Spanish dons, there has been evolved—with the exception of the skyscraper—the most distinctive type of architecture ever developed in America—the California Mission type."[17] For California schools these same comments could be made. Ideas gained through a multi-dimensional fascination with the missions, Ramona's Home, and the Mission Revival left their own heritage; it can only be seen as American and remains visually in many modern plans.

Many architects and designers were drawn to the Mission Revival as a result of its progressive possibilities, its appropriateness to site, function, and materials. As time separated the avant-garde from a mission style, others came to realize that the future would not be dependent on revivals of the past. At the climax of serious debate, architect John Galen Howard closed the issue of style for many. "If it grow naturally out of the conditions of this wonderful country and if we provide for it an environment and a nourishment of genuine feeling, it should be the finest style the world had yet seen."[18] It was the very complexity of a style like the Mission Revival that helped define the modern period. Revival or precursor of modernity? California's Mission Revival had been both.

Afterword

169

At the turn of the century architect Frederick L. Roehrig designed a mansion in Altadena for Chicago publisher Daniel Ross Cameron. Doubtless Cameron had visited the mission style California Building at the Columbian Exposition in 1893 — and, doubtless also, he was well aware of the promotional hyperbole following the Southern California land boom of the late 1880s. He, in fact, fit the stereotype. For in 1896 he purchased property for a winter residence in the young Los Angeles-Pasadena suburb of Altadena. On the eve of 1897 Cameron let the contracts for the $10,000 stucco-on-frame structure with tile roof, to be completed within the next six months. In 1899 the International Edition of *American Architect and Building News* then featured his Mission Revival mansion as one of their select representative examples of the new style. As the revival became popular with a middle class audience, other authors selected the D. R. Cameron House for their own purposes. In particular, Maurice Sloan, writing for the American Portland Cement Association, illustrated it (without identifying label) in his book of 1912: *The Concrete House and Its Construction.*

But then came the climax: Daniel Ross Cameron retired to Southern California, dying there in 1918. By 1921, his estate was offered for sale — with residence remodeled by Los Angeles architect Elmer Grey. Architects and clients alike had abused the Mission Revival during Cameron's latter years, and by the time of his death the style was certainly no longer fashionable. Grey's remodeling was saturated with irony: Grey himself had been a prominent Mission Revival proponent, 1900-10. Grey's 1920s disapproval of the earlier revival — almost caustic in its overtones — symbolized the reactions of other architects as well, and foreshadowed interpretations for decades to come.

169 Frederick L. Roehrig, Daniel Ross Cameron House, Altadena, 1897. Published in *American Architect and Building News*, International Edition, February 18, 1899. (Avery Architectural Library)
Here within the history of a single structure lies an encapsulation of the complexities of California's Mission Revival.

170 Elmer Grey, remodeling of Cameron House, Altadena, 1921. Published in *California Southland*, October 1921.
Elmer Grey's "Spanish Modern" remodeling (a combined Spanish Colonial Revival and Deco) hid forever Roehrig's original work.

170

Notes

Chapter One

Mission Imagery Romanticized

[1] Sunset, *The California Missions*, Menlo Park, CA, 1964, 221; F. Walker, *San Francisco's Literary Frontier*, New York, 1939, 128-29.

[2] During the eighteenth century concepts of the sublime became central to both real and literary buildings. Edmund Burke's notion of "pleasing gloom" preoccupied professional circles. With the writings of John Ruskin in the mid-nineteenth century, architects associated a brooding melancholy with massive, impenetrable forms. It was Ruskin, too, who further analyzed architecture to define the picturesque. Irregularity of mass and detail, dappled light, and overgrown foliage all created a romantic picture that captured not just the profession, but also the public.

[3] B. Truman, *Semi-Tropical California*, San Francisco, 1874, 134-35 [Bancroft]. Also, B. Truman, *Occidental Sketches*, San Francisco, 1881, 206 [Stanford].

[4] W. H. Bishop, "Southern California, III," *Harper's*, December 1882, 63; J. G. Oakley, "A Romance of the Mission," *Overland Monthly*, April 1883, 390; E. Roberts, "Two Seaports of New Spain," Ibid., December 1884, 572; E. Roberts, "Santa Barbara," *London Art Journal*, January 1887, 12 [Stanford].

[5] C. W. Stoughton, "The Mission Dolores," *American Architect and Building News*, March 15, 1884, 129. *American Architect and Building News* will henceforth be abbreviated as *AABN*. Truman, *Occidental Sketches*, 207.

[6] Truman, *Semi-Tropical California*, 159-60. Also G. H. Fitch, "Colony Life in Southern California," *Cosmopolitan*, November 1886, 156, and W. H. Bishop, *Mexico, California and Arizona*, New York, 1883, 440 [San Francisco Public Library; UCLA Special Collections]; *All About Santa Barbara*, n.p., 1878, 27 [Bancroft]; F. F. Victor, "Studies of the California Missions, III," *The Californian*, July 1882, 19.

[7] A. M. Manning, "San Carlos de Monterey," *Overland Monthly*, July 1884, 43-44; M. Graham, "San Carlos—Mission del Carmelo," Ibid., September 1884, 293.

[8] E. Roberts, *Santa Barbara and Around There*, Boston, 1886, 64 [San Francisco Public Library]; C.F. Holder, *Southern California, A Guidebook*, Los Angeles, 1888, 90 [California Historical Society, San Francisco]; Pasadena Board of Trade, *Pasadena and Environments*, Pasadena, 1894 [Huntington].

[9] H. H. Jackson, "Father Junipero and His Work," *Century*, May 1883, 10, 211-12.

[10] C. McWilliams, *Southern California Country*, Santa Barbara, 1973, 73-74.

[11] H. H. Jackson, *Ramona*, Pasadena Edition, 1907, 81.

[12] Jackson, "Father Junipero," *Century*, 18. *Moorish* as a descriptive term had appeared prior to Mrs. Jackson's publication of *Ramona* in 1884, but only in isolated regional literature. *California As It Is* [UC Berkeley], a guidebook published in San Francisco in 1882, discussed San Buenaventura as the "old mission church, surmounted by its Moorish towers." (56) In *Santa Barbara As It Is*, published in that city in 1884, the local mission was cited as an object of interest, being of "striking Moorish architecture." (50) [Bancroft] Mrs. Jackson's writings, however, popularized the idea that Moorish architecture truly existed in the West.

[13] G. S. Berstein, "In Pursuit of the Exotic: Islamic Form in Nineteenth Century American Architecture," Dissertation, University of Pennsylvania, 1968, 33-42, 44. During the 1830s-60s painters including Delacroix, Gerome, Courbet, and Manet had borrowed Islamic and Spanish themes for their subjects. Literature, too, had adopted Eastern tales to great effect during the eighteenth and nineteenth centuries, editions of the *Arabian Nights* being among the most popular. For Americans, it was Washington Irving's *The Alhambra: A Series of Tales and Sketches of the Moors and Spaniards* of 1832 that introduced the term *Moorish*.

[14] R. W. Gibson, "Spanish Architecture, I-XIX," *AABN*, October 1883-August 1884.

[15] S. Baxter, "Strolls About Mexico, III," *AABN*, August 16, 1884, 78.

[16] Stoughton, "Mission Dolores," *AABN*, 128; I. K. Pond, "Saunterings in Spain," *Inland Architect and News Record*, April 1884, 34. *Inland Architect and News Record* will henceforth be abbreviated as *IANR*. "Architecture of Spain," *AABN*, December 21, 1889, 291.

[17] H. C. Ford, *Etchings of the Franciscan Missions of California*, New York, 1883 [Bancroft]. Henry Chapman Ford Material, Southwest Museum, Los Angeles. Thanks go to Norman Neuerberg for alerting the author to the Southwest Museum Collection. N. Neuerberg, "Ford Drawings at the Southwest Museum," *The Masterkey*, April-June 1980, 60-64. For Ariana Day, "Restorations on Canvas," San Francisco *Bulletin*, April 15, 1882, 2.

[18] A similar phenomenon occurred in 1840s Britain. See J. Steegman, *Victorian Taste*, Cambridge, MA, 1971, 90ff. C. F. Holder, *All About Pasadena*, Boston and New York, 1889, 45, 118 [Huntington]; J. Steele, *Old California Days*, Chicago, 1889, 9 [Bancroft; California Historical Society, San Francisco].

[19] W. B. Tyler, *Old Missions, California*, San Francisco, 1890, 3 [California Historical Society, San Francisco]; J. T. Doyle, "The Missions of Alta California," *Century*, January 1891, 402; M. A. Graham, *Historical Reminiscences of One Hundred Years Ago*, San Francisco, 1876, iv [Bancroft]; P. J. Thomas, *Our Centennial Memoir*, San Francisco, 1877, 7 [Bancroft; San Francisco Public Library]; F. H. Mandeville, *Tourists' Guide to San Diego and Vicinity*, San Diego, 1888, 2 [Bancroft]. Attitudes had vacillated throughout the 1880s. See B. Harrison, "Española and Its Environs," *Harper's*, May 1885, 833; S. Storey, *To the Golden Land*, London, 1889, 66 [California Historical Society, San Francisco]. Also Steele, *California Days*, 48.

[20] N.V.S., "Junipero Serra: The Founder of the Missions," San Francisco *Chronicle*, February 6, 1882, 3. Prior to the 1880s the missions were badly neglected. At San Juan Capistrano, local citizens had used the chapel for hay storage, while at San Miguel, a saloon and sewing machine company occupied the monks' living quarters. See N. G. Weinberg, "Historic Preservation Tradition in California's Restoration of the Missions and the Spanish Colonial Revival," Dissertation, University of California, Davis, 1974, 86.

[21] *Centennial of Padre Junipero Serra*, Printed Proclamation, 1884; R. E. White, *Padre Junipero Serra and the Mission Church of San Carlos del Carmelo*, San Francisco, 1884, 13 [Bancroft]. "Restoration! vs. Ruins of Carmel Mission Church," *California Architect and Building News*, November 1884, 198. *California Architect and Building News* will henceforth be abbreviated as *CABN*.

[22] J. J. O'Keefe, *The Buildings and Churches of the Mission of Santa Barbara*, Santa Barbara, 1886 [Bancroft; Huntington]; E. S. Cummins, "The California Ranch," *Cosmopolitan*, November 1887, 215-24. From June 1885 until May 1888, no significant articles appeared in the *Times*. After this date the shift in interest may be attributed to owner Harrison Gray Otis and to the influence of Charles Fletcher Lummis.

[23] W. B. Tyler, *Old California Missions*, San Francisco, 1889 [Bancroft; UCLA Special Collections]; C. F. Lummis, "The Old Missions," *Drake's Magazine*, March 1889, 191. In 1888, Tessa L. Kelso, of the Los Angeles Public Library, established the Association for the Preservation of the Missions, while at the same time the Native Sons of the Golden West started landmarks work. Unfortunately, the hopes of these organizations were premature, for by 1895 Miss Kelso's association had collected only $90, accomplishing no actual repairs. See D. C. Gordon, *Junipero Serra; California's First Citizen*, Los Angeles, 1969, 38, and E. R. Bingham, *Charles F. Lummis; Editor of the Southwest*, San Marino, CA, 1955, 110.

[24] C. H. Shinn, "The Missions of California," *Illustrated American*, July 26, 1890, 42.

[25] See K. Starr, *Americans and the California Dream, 1850-1915*, New York, 1973, for a general account. Also G. S. Dumke, *The Boom of the Eighties in Southern California*, San Marino, CA, 1944; J. E. Baur, *The Health-Seekers of Southern California, 1870-1900*, San Marino, CA, 1959; C. D. Willard, *The Herald's History of Los Angeles City*, Los Angeles, 1901.

[26] Los Angeles *Times*, November 16, 1886, 2; December 14, 1886, 6; August 12, 1887, 10.

[27] G. W. James, *Through Ramona's Country*, Boston, 1909, 94ff; "To Camulos," Los Angeles *Times*, December 18, 1886, 4; Southern Pacific Company, *From the Crescent City to the Golden Gate via the Sunset Route*, San Francisco, 1890, 20 [Bancroft]; George E. Place Company, *Southern California Tourists' Guidebook*, Los Angeles, 1888 [Bancroft; California Historical Society, San Francisco]; Southern Pacific Company, *Southern Pacific Sketchbook*, San Francisco, 1890 [Huntington]; E. McD. Johnstone, *By Semi-Tropic Seas; Santa Barbara and Surroundings*, Buffalo, NY, 1888 [Bancroft].

[28] "Good Roads Tour, 1912," Photograph Files, California Department of Transportation, Sacramento. Thanks go to John W. Snyder for uncovering this information.

[29] D. Gunn, *San Diego*, San Diego, 1887, 103 [UCLA Special Collections]; *Southern California Tourists' Guidebook*; N. Eames, "Autumn Days in Ventura, 1," *Overland Monthly*, December 1889, 562.

[30] C. F. Lummis, *The Old Missions*, Los Angeles, 1888 [Southwest Museum, Los Angeles].

[31] F. Walker, *A Literary History of Southern California*, Berkeley, 1950, 132; C. F. Lummis, "Missions," *Drake's Magazine*, 193 and 195; C. F. Lummis, "In the Lion's Den," *Land of Sunshine*, December 1895, 43-44; C. F. Lummis, *Southern California, Land of Sunshine*, New York, 1916 [UCLA Special Collections]; C. F. Lummis, *Stand Fast Santa Barbara*, Santa Barbara, 1923 and 1927, 10, and *The Spanish Pioneers*, Chicago, 1929; Gordon, *Junipero Serra*, 55. Lummis perfected this aphorism over a thirty-six year period. In his 1893 *Spanish Pioneers* he had written, "In 1617—three years before Plymouth Rock—there were already *eleven* churches [missionary churches] in use in New Mexico." (161) It was characteristic of Lummis to rework and republish his ideas.

[32] M. P. Carroll, "The Influence of the Missions on Present-day California," Newman Prize Essay, Berkeley, 1916, 12 [Bancroft]; *Overland Monthly*, July 1895, 9, and, *Land of Sunshine*, January 1897, advertisements.

[33] Both were published in San Francisco, the latter in two volumes.

[34] See F. J. Weber, *A Select Bibliography: the California Missions, 1765-1972*, Los Angeles, 1972, for an annotated listing for the 1890s.

[35] *Land of Sunshine*, 1894-99, advertisements, *passim*; "The Landmarks Club," *Land of Sunshine*, June 1897, 26, and "Art and Artists," Los Angeles *Times*, March 18, 1890, 1; R. I. Mahood, *Photographer of the Southwest, Adam Clark Vroman, 1856-1916*, Los Angeles, 1961; "Camulos: The Real Home of Helen Hunt Jackson's Ramona," Los Angeles *Times*, January 18, 1887, 2; "Chit...Chat," *Overland Monthly*, March 1896, 352.

[36] Roberts, *Santa Barbara and Around There*, 151; *CABN*, July 1893, 76.

[37] J. G. Borglum, "An Artist's Paradise," *Land of Sunshine*, November 1894, 106; E. Neuhaus, *William Keith: The Man and the Artist*, New York, 1938, 23; Shinn, "The Missions," *Illustrated American*, 40.

Chapter Two

An Architecture of California

[1] *All About Santa Barbara*, Santa Barbara, 1878, 50-52 [Bancroft].

[2] L. Salvator, *Eine Blume aus dem goldenen Lande oder Los Angeles*, Prague, 1878, and *Los Angeles in Sudcalifornien, Eine Blume aus dem goldenen Lande*, Würzburg, Vienna, 1885. *Eine Blume* (1878), 55, 56. Author's translation [Bancroft].

[3] R. W. C. Farnsworth, *A Southern California Paradise*, Pasadena, 1883, 69-74 [Bancroft].

[4] S. Power, "Pacific Houses and Homes, I," *Overland Monthly*, October 1883, 394.

[5] S. Newsom, *California Homes*, San Francisco, 1884-89, 23 [California Historical Society, San Francisco]; W. H. Bishop, "Southern California, I," *Harper's*, October 1882, 717.

[6] K. Weitze, "Stanford and the California Missions," *The Founders and the Architects*, Stanford, 1976, 69-81; Stanford University Archives, Scrapbook #9, 93, 95-96.

[7] O. L. Elliott, *Stanford University, The First Twenty-Five Years*, Stanford, 1937, 588-92, 598; Stanford University Archives, Scrapbook #9, 128-30. Descriptions vary. See also Scrapbooks #1, 9, 13, 33A.

[8] Carnall-Hopkins Co., *Souvenir of Leland Stanford Junior University*, San Francisco, 1888, 10 [Huntington].

[9] Southern Pacific Company, *California Resorts*, San Francisco, 1897 [Bancroft].

[10] Letter from Leland Stanford to David Starr Jordan, August 24, 1892, Stanford Archives, SC 33a, Box 2, Folder 4; Weitze, "Stanford," *The Founders and the Architects*, 70-73; Letter from R. U. Johnson of the Editorial Department, *Century*, to Mr. Olmsted, December 17, 1890, Library of Congress, Olmsted Material.

[11] R. Koch, *Louis C. Tiffany, Rebel in Glass*, New York, 1964, 70; K. H. Cardwell, *Bernard Maybeck; Artisan, Architect, Artist*, Santa Barbara, 1977, 21-23; G. S. Berstein, "In Pursuit of the Exotic: Islamic Form in Nineteenth Century American Architecture," Dissertation, University of Pennsylvania, 1968, 149.

[12] The number of nonarchitects listing themselves for single commissions in *CABN* climbed radically in 1887, peaking in 1891. Indicative of the depressed building industry, these padded business entries were intended to encourage potential clients. J. W. Snyder, manuscript revision of "Index of San Francisco Building, 1879-1900," Master's Thesis, University of California, Davis, 1975, in process, 1982.

[13] B. McDougall and Son were in San Diego in 1884, 1888-89; Willis Polk, Los Angeles, 1887-88; John Galen Howard, Los Angeles, 1887-88; William P. Moore, Los Angeles, 1884; Ernest Coxhead, Los Angeles, 1887-88; John C. Pelton, Los Angeles, Riverside, and San Diego, 1887-88; W. J. Cuthbertson, Los Angeles, 1885-89; Joseph Cather Newsom, Los Angeles, 1887-88. See Snyder, "Index," 1975, and the *Los Angeles City Directories*, 1886/87-1891.

[14] In Los Angeles, John Galen Howard worked first for Caukin and Haas and then for James M. Wood from August 1887 to September 1888. These men, like Shepley, Rutan and Coolidge, designed in a Richardsonian Romanesque style. Howard and Polk apparently met in June 1888, immediately after Howard began working for Wood. See J.E. Draper, "John Galen Howard and the Beaux-Arts Movement in the United States," Master's Thesis, Architecture, University of California, Berkeley, 1972, 33-35, and John Galen Howard, 1864-1931, Correspondence c.1873-1932, Bancroft Library, Box 7-12, Letters of 1887-88. In particular, letter from Howard to his mother, Los Angeles, June 3, 1888. Thanks go to Joan E. Draper for her assistance.

[15] The drawing itself is evidently lost. Only a published copy cut from *Architecture and Building* of April 19, 1890, exists in a Willis Polk Album held in the Documents Collection, College of Environmental Design, University of California, Berkeley.

[16] W. Polk, "An Imaginary Mission Church of Southern California Type," dated 1887, published in *Architecture and Building*, April 19, 1890, 186-87.

[17] J. G. Howard, Sketchbook, 1884-89, in John Galen Howard Correspondence, Bancroft Library, Carton I.

[18] Howard Correspondence, Bancroft Library, letter from John Galen Howard to his mother, Los Angeles, March 5, 1888. Also see letters from Howard to his mother, Los Angeles, October 5, 1887, March 27, 1888, and September 2, 1888.

[19] In *CABN*: S. Newsom, "Alhambra Cottage," January 15, 1889, 8; "Precita," March 15, 1889, 36; "Rio Dell Cottage," April 15, 1889. The latter design is unsigned, but is apparently Newsom's. Also in *CABN*: S. Newsom, untitled design, November 1889, 147; "Un Chateau en Espagne," February 1891.

[20] "Prospectus of First Year," *Architectural News*, November 1890, v [Environmental Design Library, University of California, Berkeley].

[21] H. Kirker, *California's Architectural Frontier*, Santa Barbara, 1973, 122. "Old California Missions, I," *Architectural News*, November 1890, 9 [Environmental Design Library, University of California, Berkeley].

[22] R. M. Turner, "An Adobe Mission Church," *Architectural News*, November 1890 [Environmental Design Library, University of California, Berkeley].

[23] C. D. Warner, "The Winter of Our Content," *Harper's*, December 1890, 48-49.

[24] H. T. B., "Old Mission Church at Sonoma, California," *CABN*, January 1891, 3; February 1891, 15-16; March 1891, 27; April 1891, 39. Also *CABN*: Tres, "Old Mission Dolores Church, San Francisco, Cal.," May 1891, 51; "Mission of San Carlos del Carmelo, Cal.," June 1891, 63-64; "Mission of San Antonio, Cal.," July 1891, 75-76; "Mission of San Miguel, Cal.," August 1891, 87; "The Old Church of Monterey and the Mission of Sant Inez," September 1891, 99-100; "The Mission of Santa Barbara," October 1891, 111-12; "Ventura Mission," November 1891, 123; "Mission Fragments," December 1891, 136.

[25] C. A. Rich, "A Run Through Spain, V," *AABN*, February 7, 1891, 87-88. Also *AABN*, February-September, 1891, *passim*. H. Saladin, "Spanish Architecture, I-V," *AABN*, April-June 1891, *passim*.

[26] World's Fair Matters," San Francisco *Call*, April 17, 1891, 1; California World's Fair Commission, *California's Monthly World's Fair Magazine*, May 1891, 19 [Bancroft; California State Library, Sacramento. The Sacramento collection holds the complete eight-issue set: May-June 1891, and January-June 1892. A publication hiatus occurred during the latter six months of 1891].

[27] "For the Big Show," San Francisco *Call*, June 4, 1891, 2; "The World's Fair," San Francisco *Chronicle*, June 4, 1891, 12; "California's Building," San Francisco *Examiner*, June 4, 1891, 3; "Nine Competitions," Los Angeles *Herald*, June 4, 1891, 1. See also "Proposed California Building," *World's Fair Magazine*, June 1891, 15-19 [California State Library, Sacramento].

[28] "California's Building," *Examiner*, 3; "For the Big Show," *Call*, 2.

[29] "For the Big Show," *Call*, 2.

[30] See Note 27. Also "Another Plan," San Francisco *Examiner*, June 5, 1891, 6.

[31] "The World's Fair," San Francisco *Chronicle*, June 10, 1891, 10; "World's Fair Work," Los Angeles *Herald*, June 10, 1891, 1; "The World's Fair Work of the California Commissioners," San Francisco *Chronicle*, June 12, 1891, 2; "Preparing for the Fair," Chicago *Tribune*, June 14, 1891, 6; "State Building Plans," Chicago *Tribune*, June 20, 1891, 9.

[32] Chicago Inter-Ocean, "The World's Fair. The Texas Building," San Francisco *Chronicle*, August 5, 1891, 1; T. Hines, *Burnham of Chicago*, New York, 1974, 96.

[33] "California to Beat the World," San Francisco *Call*, August 16, 1891, 3; "California Building," Los Angeles *Times*, August 30, 1891, 1; "California At the World's Fair," San Francisco *Call*, October 4, 1891, 10; E. W. Keeler, *America Focalized*, and *California For Worldly Eyes in 1893*, San Francisco, 1891 [Bancroft]; M. H. DeYoung, "California's Opportunity," *The Californian*, October 1891, 18, 20.

[34] "Preparing to Exhibit," Los Angeles *Times*, December 2, 1891, 5; "The World's Fair. Reports Read by the Delegates," San Francisco *Chronicle*, December 11, 1891, 1; "The World's Fair...Unique Decorations," San Francisco *Chronicle*, December 20, 1891, 17; W. J. Cuthbertson, "California World's Fair Building," *CABN*, December 1891, 138; E. Peixotto, *The Wave*, December 19, 1891 [Bancroft].

[35] "Moorish-Mission," San Francisco *Chronicle*, January 13, 1892, 10.

[36] "Working on the Fair," San Francisco *Examiner*, January 13, 1892, 4; "World's Fair. The California Commission Again in Session," San Francisco *Call*, January 13, 1892, 3.

[37] "Our Chicago Exhibit," San Francisco *Chronicle*, January 14, 1892, 12; "A State Building," San Francisco *Call*, January 21, 1892, 3; "The State Building," San Francisco *Chronicle*, January 21, 1892, 5; "California's Building," San Francisco *Examiner*, January 21, 1892, 4. "Instructions," *California's Monthly World's Fair Magazine*, January 1892, 55-56 [Bancroft]. See also "The California State Building," *CABN*, January 1892, 2.

[38] "California's Exhibition Building," *California's Monthly World's Fair Magazine*, February 1892, 59-63 [Bancroft]. Those architects listed where W. G. Mitchel and A. G. Daw, San Francisco; B. McDougall and Son, Plan 1 and 2, San Francisco; Ferris and Boswell, Monterey; S. I. Haas, Los Angeles; Maxwell G. Bugbee, San Francisco; Copeland and Peirce, San Francisco; Edward Larsen, San Francisco; W. W. Polk, San Francisco; Daniel Polk, San Francisco; Oliver Everett, San Francisco; A. Page Brown, San Francisco; Albert Pissis and W. P. Moore, San Francisco; Alfred Gould, San Francisco; Coxhead and Coxhead, San Francisco; Edward Burns, San Francisco; John C. Pelton, San Francisco; Newton J. Tharp, San Francisco; J. Ray, San Francisco; Mooser and Cuthbertson, San Francisco; Samuel Newsom, Plans 1-4, San Francisco; Eugene L. Caukin, Los Angeles; J. B. Mathison, Plan 1 and 2, San Francisco; Stuart F. Smith, Oakland; C. L. Strange, Los Angeles; E. W. Keeler, San Francisco. Second place went to B. McDougall and Son; third to John C. Pelton; fourth to Samuel Newsom; fifth to Albert Pissis and W. P. Moore. (Notably all had been represented in Southern California, 1884-87.) Evidently Bernard Maybeck worked with J. B. Mathison on one design. See "San Francisco...Competitions for the State Building," *AABN*,

March 19, 1892, 187-88. See also *Biennial Report, California World's Fair Commission*, 1892 [Bancroft].

[39] Architects adopted the quatrefoil window as typifying a mission style. This motif was only rarely used in California Franciscan architecture—apparently only at San Carlos de Borromeo and San Rafael Arcángel. As one of the most sculptured elements of mission design, the quatrefoil derived from the Baroque Spanish traditions of Mexico and Texas.

[40] "California's Exhibition Building," *World's Fair Magazine*, February 1892, 62 [Bancroft]; "Accepted Plans," San Francisco *Call*, February 12, 1892, 8; "The World's Fair," San Francisco *Chronicle*, February 12, 1892, 8; "California at the Fair," San Francisco *Examiner*, February 12, 1892, 5; *The Wave*, February 13, 1892, 7 [Bancroft].

[41] "Design of California's Building," Chicago *Tribune*, February 20, 1892, 12; "San Francisco: Competitions," *AABN*, March 19, 1892, 187-188.

[42] *Final Report of the California World's Fair Commission*, Sacramento, 1894, 12.

Chapter Three

A Modern Mission Style

[1] P. V. Turner, "The Collaborative Design of Stanford University," *The Founders and the Architects*, Stanford, 1976, 53ff. The California State Library, Sacramento, holds an incomplete run of *Transactions*. Thanks go to John W. Snyder for his discovery of this journal.

[2] "The First Annual Exhibition," *CABN*, April 1894, 38.

[3] Pasadena Board of Trade, "Some Houses Erected in 1893," *Pasadena and Environments*, Pasadena, 1894 [Huntington]; T. W. Parkes, "House of Mrs. Edwin Greble, Pasadena, Cal.," *AABN*, February 11, 1899.

[4] Pasadena Board of Trade, *Pasadena, 1892, Crown of the Valley*, Los Angeles, 23 [UCLA Special Collections]; "Hotel Green, Pasadena," *CABN*, November 1898, 128-30. (This article discusses the 1898 addition, Mission Revival in style, by Frederick L. Roehrig. In giving a history of the hotel, it was cited that a previous annex had been added in 1890. This must be an error. The 1892 addition by C. L. Strange was the first annex to the hotel after Colonel Green's purchase in 1888. As a result of the misdating by *CABN*, and through a confusion of the 1892 and 1898 annexes with one another, several secondary sources have mistakenly discussed the Hotel Green as an 1890 Mission Revival design by Frederick L. Roehrig. Today the 1888-92 sections of the hotel no longer exist. However, the 1898-1901 additions survive as the Green Apartments.) Ledger Publishing Company, *A General Historical, Statistical and Descriptive Review of Pasadena, California, and Suburbs*, Los Angeles, 1893, 60; "The Hotel Green," Pasadena *Crown Vista*, January 6, 1894, 1; and, *Pasadena and Environments*, 1894 [Huntington].

[5] San Mateo County *Times-Gazette*, April 23, 1892, 3; B. McDougall and Son, "Gateway, Cypress Lawn Cemetery," *CABN*, September 1896, 105; Thomas P. Ross, "Columbarium," Ibid., February 1894; Belmont School, San Francisco, 1892-93 [California State Library, Sacramento]; "Improvements at Belmont," San Francisco *Call*, June 30, 1893, 6.

[6] Address of James D. Phelan, *Literary and Other Exercises in the California State Building*, Chicago, 1893, 22-23 [Bancroft]; Rand, McNally and Company, *Handbook of the World's Columbian Exposition*, Chicago, 1893, 183 [San Francisco Public Library]; W. B. Robinson, *Texas Public Buildings of the Nineteenth Century*, Austin, 1974, 113-14.

[7] *Official Portfolio of the California Midwinter International Exposition*, San Francisco, 1894 [Bancroft].

[8] "Fair Buildings," San Francisco *Call*, August 3, 1893, 3. Also "Architectural Suggestions for the Midwinter Fair Buildings," San Francisco *Call*, August 6, 1893, 8-9. The first article discusses designs by A. Page Brown, Samuel Newsom, Edward R. Swain, B. G. McDougall, and Willis Polk. The second lists the submitted sets of drawings, describing each architect's use of style:

Leo Bonet and Fransquin Arveuf (Moorish); A. Page Brown (Spanish-Moorish); William Mooser and Morin Goustiaux (no style given); Edward R. Swain (East Indian, Mission, others); Edmund Kollofrath (Oriental, Moorish); M. G. Bugbee (Mission); Alexander F. Oakey, C. J. Colley and Emil S. Lemme (Moorish); anonymous set attributed to Willis Polk (Mission); B. G. McDougall (Moorish, Egyptian, others); J. Gash (no style given; glass building proposed); W. Jones Cuthbertson (Spanish); Clarkson Swain (no style given); Samuel Newsom (Mission); J. Murray (Spanish); E. A. Harrison ("Mission and Moorish, the whole commonly included in the term Spanish"); and Herbert B. Maggs (no style given). Several sketches of the proposed buildings accompanied the August 6 article. With the exception of the Oakey, Colley and Lemme design, these were reprinted at later dates as the winning designs. See also "A Unique Scheme," San Francisco *Call*, August 15, 1893, 10.

[9] *CABN*, September 1893, 102-03; K. H. Cardwell, *Bernard Maybeck; Artisan, Architect, Artist*, Santa Barbara, 1977, 29. A. Page Brown's coterie of draftsmen brings up additional issues of attribution. *American Builders Review* credits Albert C. Schweinfurth with much of the Spanish design work claimed by Brown, including "some of the buildings of the Midwinter Fair." See "Local Examples of Spanish Renaissance," *American Builders Review*, September 1906, 247 [California State Library, Sacramento]. *American Builders Review* will henceforth be abbreviated as *ABR*. Again, thanks go to John W. Snyder for his discovery of this journal.

[10] P. Weaver, Jr., "The California Midwinter International Exposition," *Overland Monthly*, November 1893, 456 and 461.

[11] Ibid., 462; *Official Portfolio*, 1894; "For Los Angeles," San Francisco *Call*, October 13, 1893, 4; "California's Midwinter International Exposition," San Francisco *Chronicle*, December 31, 1893, 5; "Taber's Photographic Gallery," *CABN*, April 1894; F. Wiggins, "The Midwinter Fair," *Land of Sunshine*, July 1894, 38; *Official Guide to the California Midwinter Exposition*, 1st Edition, San Francisco, 1894, 57, 105, 119 [Bancroft].

[12] The official portfolio of the Midwinter Fair noted that it included both "French and Spanish" details as well as "the features of old Mission buildings." *Official Portfolio*, 1894. "The Midwinter Fair," Pasadena *Crown Vista*, December 9, 1893, 5 [Huntington]; *Land of Sunshine*, June 1894, 12.

[13] "San Francisco. The Midwinter Fair," *AABN*, November 4, 1893, 59; *CABN*, January 1894; *IANR*, June 1894.

[14] Southern Pacific Company, *California for Health, Pleasure and Profit*, San Francisco, 1894, 104 [Bancroft].

[15] N. G. Weinberg, "Historic Preservation Tradition in California's Restoration of the Missions and the Spanish Colonial Revival," Dissertation, University of California, Davis, 1974, 110; *La Fiesta de Los Angeles*, Los Angeles, 1894, and Ibid., Los Angeles, 1895 [UCLA Special Collections]; F. Van Vleck, "La Fiesta de Los Angeles, 1895," *Land of Sunshine*, April 1895, 83-84; "Glimpses of La Fiesta de Los Angeles, April 1895," Ibid., May 1895, Supplement; F. Walker, *A Literary History of Southern California*, Berkeley, 1950, 143-44.

[16] The Newsom brothers designed the California Building for the Louisiana Purchase Exposition. See San Francisco Architectural Club, *Catalogue of the Second Annual Exhibition*, San Francisco, 1903, 271. Also C. E. Hodges, "Sketch for California Building, London, England," *Architect and Engineer*, July 1911, 76. *Architect and Engineer* will henceforth be abbreviated as *AE*. (This journal was sometimes also titled *Architect and Engineer of California*.)

[17] A. C. Schweinfurth, "Hacienda del Oso, Sunol, Cal.," *AABN*, May 2, 1896; "Obituary—A. C. Schweinfurth," *AABN*, October 20, 1900, 22. Schweinfurth had worked under A. Page Brown at the time of the California Building competition. S. Newsom, J. M. Lane House and "Residence for Mr. Parker, Marinita Park, San Rafael," *CABN*, May and September 1897. J. Murray, "Country Residence," and Havens and Toepke, untitled design, *CABN*, November 1898.

[18] G. W. James, "The Influence of the 'Mission Style' Upon the Civic and Domestic Architecture of Modern California," *Craftsman*, February 1904, 466-68.

[19] C. F. Lummis, "The Lesson of Adobe," *Land of Sunshine*, March 1895, 66. Also published in Pasadena Board of Trade, *Illustrated Souvenir Book*, Pasadena, 1897 [Huntington] and *AABN*, May 8, 1899.

[20] "La Mita," and "Gail Borden Residence," *Land of Sunshine*, May 1896, 295, 301; R. L. Makinson, *Greene and Greene; Architecture as a Fine Art*, Salt Lake City, 1977, 44; C. S. Greene, "California Home Making," Pasadena *Star*, January 1, 1905.

[21] E. A. Otis, "Characteristic Homes," Los Angeles *Times*, January 1, 1897, 12 and "Santa Barbara," Ibid., April 18, 1887, 6.

[22] S. P. Hunt, "Architecture," Los Angeles *Times*, January 1, 1897, 13.

[23] Otis, "Homes," *Times*, 1897; Pasadena Board of Trade, *Illustrated Souvenir Book*, Pasadena, 1898 [Huntington].

[24] Blick and Moore, "House of Frank Emery, Esq., Pasadena, Cal.," *AABN*, February 18, 1899; "Residence in Imitation of Early Mission Style," Los Angeles *Times*, January 1, 1899, Pt. II, 9; "A Pasadena House in the Mission Style," *House and Garden*, April 1905, 208.

[25] J. P. Kremple, "Houses, Old and New," Los Angeles *Times*, January 1, 1898, 22-24.

[26] Pasadena Board of Trade, *Illustrated Souvenir Book*, 1898; Blick and Moore, "House of H. B. Sherman, Pasadena, Cal.," *AABN*, International Edition, February 18, 1899 [Avery Library].

[27] Several sources date the row to 1894-95. (H. Andree, *Santa Barbara Architecture, from Spanish Colonial to Modern*, Santa Barbara, 1975, 70; D. Gebhard, *A Guide to Architecture in Los Angeles and Southern California*, Santa Barbara, 1977, 547.) Yet both regional and architectural periodicals illustrate the Crocker residences in 1898-1900. (*AABN*, Imperial Edition, January 15, 1898; *House Beautiful*, December 1898; *Land of Sunshine*, March 1900.) The 1898-1900 photographs show the structures as either unfinished or only recently completed. To further complicate matters, A. Page Brown died in February 1896. He may have seen the commission through, or it may have been completed by someone in his office—possibly A. C. Schweinfurth.

[28] A. Page Brown, "Cottages for W.H. Crocker, Esq. Near Mission Gardens, Santa Barbara, Cal.," *AABN*, Imperial Edition, January 15, 1898, iv and viii (advertisement pages). No accompanying text. Pasadena Evening Star, *Pasadena, California, The City Beautiful*, Pasadena, 1901 [Huntington].

[29] "A Distinctive Style," Los Angeles *Times*, January 1, 1899, 9; F. L. Roehrig, "House of D. R. Cameron, Altadena, Cal.," *AABN*, International Edition, February 18, 1899 [Avery Library].

[30] E. Evans, *Burlingame, Its Railroad Station, an American Classic*, San Mateo, CA, 1971, 4-6. Also D. F. Regnery, *An Enduring Heritage: Historic Buildings of the San Francisco Peninsula*, Stanford, 1976. For San Juan Capistrano: "Autobiography of Benjamin F. Levet," typescript, Los Angeles Public Library; Southern California Railway, "San Juan Capistrano," *A Digest of Southern California*, Chicago, 1894, 23 [Stanford]. Mathison and Howard, "Burlingame Railway Station," *CABN*, April 1894, 39.

[31] S. Newsom, "Proposed Hotel near Golden Gate Park, San Francisco, California," *CABN*, May 1895; *Los Angeles of Today Architecturally* [UCLA Special Collections].

[32] "Hotel Green, Pasadena," *CABN*, November 1898, 129; "Southern California's Great Hotel Completed, the Hotel Green and Annex," *Land of Sunshine*, December 1898, advertisements; Pasadena Board of Trade, *Illustrated Souvenir Book*, Pasadena, 1903. [Los Angeles Public Library; Bancroft].

[33] *Los Angeles of Today Architecturally*; K. T. Galpin, "Our Schools," *Land of Sunshine*, September 1895, 181.

[34] "Dedication of new High School," Los Angeles *Times*, May 21, 1898, 15.

[35] In *Land of Sunshine*: T.S. Van Dyke, "San Diego, The Italy of America," November 1897, 274; C. C. Davis, "Education in Southern California," September 1898, 214; J. A. Knight, "Redlands," February 1899, 63-70. L. Burgess, *A. K. Smiley Public Library*, pamphlet, Redlands.

[36] "The Fresno Water Tower," *Fresno Past and Present*, October 1964, 1 and 4. In *CABN*: B.J. S. Cahill, "Design for N.S.G.W. Building," November 1895; E. R. Swain, "Golden Gate Park Lodge, San Francisco, 1896," June 1896; Percy and Hamilton, "Maria Kip Orphanage," September 1896; Hermann and Swain, "I.O.O.F. Orphanage, Thermalito, Butte Co., Cal.," July 1896; H. E. Brook, *The County and City of Los Angeles*, Los Angeles, 1897, 17 [Bancroft].

[37] Southern Pacific Company, *California for Health, Pleasure and Profit*, 1894, 35.

[38] L. B. Powers, *The Story of the Old Missions*, San Francisco, 1893, v-vi [California Historical Society, San Francisco]; H. E. Brook, *Land of Sunshine*, Los Angeles, 1893 [Bancroft].

[39] S. P. Hunt, "The Adobe in Architecture," *Land of Sunshine*, July 1894, 25; C. F. Lummis, "The Lesson of the Adobe," Ibid., March 1895, 65-67.

[40] C. F. Lummis, "The Patio," and "The Grand Veranda," *Land of Sunshine*, June 1895, 15, and July 1895, 65.

[41] A. B. Benton, "The Patio," and "Architecture for the Southwest," *Land of Sunshine*, August 1897, 108-12, and February 1896, 126-30; C. D. Tyng, "Lessons from the Alhambra," Ibid., April 1896, 214-21; *Los Angeles of Today Architecturally*, preface; A. V. LaMotte, "Adobe Houses for Practical Uses," *Overland Monthly*, September 1897, 239-42; G. E. Channing, "La Cabaña," *Land of Sunshine*, January 1898, 60-63; Overman, "Modern Spanish Architecture," *House Beautiful*, 33 and 36.

[42] D. C. Gordon, *Junipero Serra: California's First Citizen*, Los Angeles, 1969, 96; T. L. Fiske, *Charles F. Lummis: the Man and his West*, University of Oklahoma, 1975, 87; E. R. Bingham, *Charles F. Lummis; Editor of the Southwest*, San Marino, CA, 1955, 104; "The Landmarks Club," *Land of Sunshine*, April 1896, 233-34.

[43] A. H. Noll, "The Spanish Missions of the Pacific Coast," *AABN*, June 5, 1897, 76. See also "To Preserve the California Mission Buildings," Ibid., July 25, 1896, 32. P. N. Boeringer, "Preserve the Missions," *Overland Monthly*, January 1897, 105-06; Fiske, *Lummis*, 91.

Chapter Four

The Mission Revival Comes of Age

[1] L. C. Davis, "A Passing View of Some Local Happenings," Stockton *Mail*, October 21, 1899, 2; S. Comstock, "The 'Dobe' of To-day," *American Homes and Gardens*, December 1906, 377.

[2] Comstock, 379; H. D. Croly, "The California Country House," *AE*, December 1906, 25.

[3] "Unique Apartment Flats," *AE*, August 1907, 56; H. Menken, *Bungalowcraft*, Los Angeles, c.1908 [Environmental Design Library, University of California, Berkeley]; W. Knowles, "The Garden and the Bungalow," *AE*, November 1906, 19; Davis, 2.

[4] "California to Have a Model Municipality," *AE*, May 1911, 57; Garden City Company of California, *Ideal Homes in Garden Communities*, New York, 1915 [California Historical Society, San Francisco; Huntington]; "Ajo, Arizona," *The Building Review*, July 1919, 5, 6, and 17, plates 8-12; "Tyrone, New Mexico, The Development of Phelps-Dodge Corporation," *Architectural Forum*, April 1918, 130-34.

[5] "Recent Tendencies in California Residence Work," *AABN*, September 7, 1910, 83 (Reprinted in *AE* the following month.); Southern Pacific Company, *California South of Tehachapi*, 8th edition, San Francisco, 1904, 101 [Bancroft]; A. S. C. Forbes, *Then and Now, 100 Landmarks within 50 Miles of Los Angeles Civic Center*, n.p., 1939.

[6] L. L. Waters, *Steel Trails to Santa Fe*, Lawrence, KA, 1950, 170; Southern Pacific Company, *Southern Pacific's First Century*, San Francisco, 1955, 29, 33, 39; A. B. Benton, "The California Mission and Its Influence Upon Pacific Coast Architecture," *AE*, February 1911, 75.

[7] Southern Pacific Company, *South of Tehachapi*, San Francisco, 1900, and *California's Coast Country*, San Francisco, 1907, 8 [Bancroft]; "Among the Architects. Building Reports," *AE*, February 1906, 90; Southern Pacific Company, *The Road of a Thousand Wonders*, San Francisco, 1907, 16 [Bancroft]; "Station, Santa Barbara, Cal.," *IANR*, February 1908; J. D. Isaacs, "Spanish Art in Texas," *Sunset*, August 1903, 384-87; F. Jennings, "Some California Railroad Stations," *AE*, February 1917, 43-54; and N. M. Stineman, "Spanish Mission Architecture in Railway Passenger Stations," *AE*, September

1920, 75-79; "Upbuilding the West, New Railway Projects," *Sunset,* October 1907, 584-86; W. H. Wheeler, "Architecture," *AE,* January 1906, 37-42.

8 Atchison, Topeka and Santa Fe, *The San Joaquin Valley,* Los Angeles, 1901, 13-14 [Bancroft]; "Hotel and Depot at Albuquerque," *AE,* August 1905, 44-45; Atchison, Topeka and Santa Fe, *California Tourist Sleeper Excursions,* Chicago, 1908 [Bancroft]; "Santa Fe Passenger Depot at Ash Fork, Ariz.," *AE,* February 1906, 88; F. S. Swales, "The Railway Hotel," *Architectural Review,* April 1913, 55; "The New Santa Fe Passenger Station, San Diego, California," *AE,* June 1914, 110.

9 S. Crump, *Western Pacific; the Railroad that was Built too Late,* Los Angeles, 1963, 20; C. W. Boynton, "Decorative Possibilities of Concrete," *AE,* April 1914, 55; W. A. Meyers and I. L. Swett, *The Story of the Los Angeles Railway, Trolleys to the Surf,* Glendale, 1976; D. Duke, *Pacific Electric Railway,* San Marino, CA, 1958; R. Long, *Pacific Electric's Big Red Cars,* Universal City, CA, 1966.

10 Subsequent to his late 1880s and early 1890s work with mission design, Polk was employed with Daniel Burnham in Chicago, 1902-04. During this time he became friends with the architect. In 1904 Polk returned to San Francisco, and was later asked to direct the West Coast office of D. H. Burnham and Company. "New Passenger and Freight Depot for the Western Pacific," *AE,* March 1910, 8; "Willis Polk," *San Francisco, Its Builders Past and Present,* Chicago and San Francisco, 1913, 275-76; T. Hines, *Burnham of Chicago; Architect and Planner,* New York, 1974, 269, 427.

11 Hunt (Sumner P.) and Eager, "Raymond Hotel, Pasadena, Cal.," *IANR,* June 1902; Sunset, *Paso Robles Hot Springs,* San Francisco, 1902, 12 [Bancroft]; Marsh and Russell, "Proposed Hotel Majestic," in M. Hume, *Los Angeles Architecturally,* Los Angeles, 1902 [Huntington]; Austin and Brown, "New Bixby Hotel, Long Beach," *AE,* April 1906, 70; Southern Pacific Company, *The San Joaquin Valley,* San Francisco, 1907-08, 16 [Bancroft]; Reid Brothers, "Hotel at Byron Hot Springs, Cal.," *AE,* November 1910, 54; E. B. Brown, "New Tourist Hotel, Stockton," *AE,* July 1908, 3, and August 1910, 19; Stone and Smith, "Mission Hotel, Santa Rosa," *AE,* January 1907, 48.

12 K. J. Weitze, "Charles Beasley, Architect (1827-1913): Issues and Images," *Journal of the Society of Architectural Historians,* October 1980, 192.

13 C. F. Whittlesey, "Hotel Wentworth, Pasadena," *AE,* March 1908, 56; J. F. Walker, "Hotel St. Anthony, San Antonio, Texas," *AABN,* September 8, 1909; "The Galvez of Galveston," *The Hotel Monthly,* March 1912, 36-48 [Rosenberg Library, Galveston, Texas].

14 Atchison, Topeka and Santa Fe, *Mission Inn,* Los Angeles, c.1910 [Bancroft]; G. Stickley, "The Colorado Desert and California," *Craftsman,* June 1904, 256; F. Walker, *A Literary History of Southern California,* Berkeley, 1950, 239, 242; M. P. Carroll, "The Influence of the Missions on Present-Day California," Newman Prize Essay, Berkeley, 1916, 13-14 [Bancroft].

15 Benton, "The California Mission," *AE,* 45-46, 75.

16 E. Grey, "Beverly Hills Hotel, Beverly Hills, California," *AE,* December 1916, 60-61; W. Knowles, "Competitive Design for Tourist Hotel at Claremont Park, Berkeley," *AE,* April 1906, 40.

17 S. McGroarty, *Mission Memories,* Los Angeles, 1929, 14; F. Rey, "A Tribute to Mission Style," *AE,* October 1924, 77-78.

18 "Architectural Suggestions," Stockton *Mail,* October 23, 1899, 4; L. C. Davis, "The Architecture of Shoolhouses," Ibid., October 31, 1899, 7; A. B. Benton, "The Cloister of Harvard School," *Architectural Record,* January 1905, 6; "20th St. School House," in *Los Angeles Architecturally*; J. L. Burton, "Long Beach School House," *AE,* February 1906, 66-67.

19 In *AE*: "Some Fresno County Architecture," June 1906, 55, 59; "Suburban Architecture in California," June 1907, 46-47; William H. Weeks, "Building the School," June 1911, 57-62; "More Honor for Architect Weeks," February 1914, 113; "The Work of William H. Weeks," May 1915, 69-78.

20 M. Hunt and E. Grey, "Two California Colleges," *AABN,* June 22, 1910, 233-36. In *AE*: "The Los Angeles Architectural Club's Annual Exhibition," July 1908, 61-62; F. S. Allen, "The Mission Type School House," September 1908, 35-43, and "The San Jose High School," March 1909, 34-45; "Unique Design for a High School Building," July 1912, 104-05. F. S. Allen, "School, National City, Cal.," *IANR,* February 1907.

21 In *AE*: F. S. Allen, "The Mission Type School House," September 1908, 35, and "The San Jose High School," 37-38; W. H. Parker, "The Requirements of a Modern School Building," March 1910, 53-63. *American Builders Review* spoofed this structural issue in a satirical essay of August 1906. Commenting on both the missions and Mission Revival: "The 'mission style' is a building that is built with earthquakes in mind—broad at the base, very simple, solid and usually but one story high. The lofty steeples, vaulted roofs, overhanging battlements and ornate features of the old world cathedrals were not repeated by these Spanish monks. They calculated on God's displeasure." The Philistine, untitled essay, *ABR,* August 1906, 230 [California State Library, Sacramento].

22 Hunt and Grey, "Two California Colleges," *AABN,* 233; Weeks, "Building the School," *AE,* June 1911, 57 and 61.

23 California Department of Instruction, *School Architecture,* Sacramento, 1909, 5 [Huntington]; R. Riordon, "A New Idea in State Schools," *Craftsman,* April 1913, 52-60.

24 School Board Journal, "California's Architectural Contribution," *AE,* March 1915, 101; "The One-Story School House," *AE,* August 1914, 69-70; H. T. Withey, "Some Phases of School-House Construction," *AABN,* November 4, 1914, 273-77; W. C. Hays, "One-Story and Open-Air Schoolhouses in California," *Architectural Forum,* July 1917, 3-12; Hays, "Concluding Paper," Ibid., September 1917, 57-66.

25 "Unique Lighting Plan of Santa Clara Grammar School," *AE,* May 1914, 90.

26 First Baptist Church, "A Proposed Design for the New Church," *Picturesque Long Beach by the Sea,* Long Beach, 1902 [Bancroft].

27 In *AE*: "Some Fresno," 55 and 57; L. S. Stone and H. C. Smith, "Masonic Building, Old Mission," December 1908, 60; L. M. Turton, "Design for Masonic Hall at Yuba City, California," October 1910, 46; "California Club's New Home," November 1905, 27; "Mission Architecture for Federal Buildings," May 1909, 108. "The Suggestive Sketch for State Street Arch," *Santa Barbara,* December 1906, 14 [Bancroft].

28 For a discussion of Mission Revival libraries, see J. H. McKay, "Some California Libraries," *ABR,* December 1905, 113-21. Like others before it, Julia Morgan's *Examiner* Building of 1912 drew upon details of the 1892 California Building.

29 In *AE*: J. Morgan, "Bell Tower of Reinforced Concrete at Mills College, Cal.," April 1908; N. F. Marsh, "Reinforced Concrete Tower, Torrey Estate, Lindsay, Cal.," December 1912, 60; Hunt and Burns, "Southwest Museum, Los Angeles," May 1913, 76. "Italian Swiss Colony's New Reinforced Concrete Champagne Building," *Cement Age,* July 1910, 6; J. B. Leonard, "Oakland Avenue Reinforced-Concrete Bridge," *Engineering News,* September 14, 1911, 303.

30 Cutter and Malmgren, "Davenport's Restaurant (Remodeled), Spokane, Wash.," *IANR,* April 1904; S. B. Newsom, "California Mission Style of Architecture Followed in Design for Eastern Chocolate Factory," *AE,* October 1912, 103; "The Concrete Stock Pavilion at the State Fair Grounds at St. Paul," *Cement Age,* May 1907, 280.

Chapter Five

Principles for a New Era

1 E. Hughes, *The California of the Padres; or, Footprints of Ancient Communism,* San Francisco, 1875, 23, 33 [San Francisco Public Library].

2 C. L. Overman, "Modern Spanish Architecture in California," *House Beautiful,* December 1898, 36.

3 C. A. Keeler, *Southern California,* Los Angeles, 1899, 129-30, 133 [UCLA Special Collections].

[4] O. Percival, "The Mexican Patio," *House Beautiful*, January 1900, 90-91; H. W. Waterman, "The Influence of an Olden Time," Ibid., June 1903, 8; "Traces of the Franciscans in California," *Craftsman*, February 1902, 29-30.

[5] "Traces," *Craftsman*, 36-37.

[6] F. J. Hunt, "The Country House and Its Style," *Craftsman*, February 1903, 283. Occasionally, an author attempted to justify the revival outside California. See H. L. Jones, "Mission Architecture in Warm and Cold Climates," *Country Life in America*, October 1903, 434-36 and, "A California Mission House That Might Be Built in the East or South," *Craftsman*, March 1909, 723-25.

[7] H. Ellis, "Sermons in Sun Dried Bricks: From the Old Spanish Missions," *Craftsman*, December 1903, 216; C. A. Keeler, *The Simple Home*, San Francisco, 1904, 34, 35 [California Historical Society, San Francisco]. See also C. Keeler, "Thoughts on Home Building in California," *AE*, October 1905, 21.

[8] In *Craftsman*: "A Craftsman House," January 1904, 399; "A California House Modeled on the Simple Lines of the Old Mission Dwelling," November 1906, 208-21; H. L. Grant, "A Mission Bungalow in Southern California," January 1909, 481-86.

[9] "A New Architecture in a New Land," *Craftsman*, August 1912, 472-73; "Concrete Cottages in California," *AE*, January 1913, 67-72; B. H. Smith, "Creating an American Style of Architecture: Mr. Gill's Distinctive Concrete Houses," *House and Garden*, July 1914, 17-20, 46; I. F. Morrow, "A Step in California's Architecture," *AE*, August 1922, 47-103H.

[10] Hunt, "The Country House," *Craftsman*, 283; G. Stickley, "A Craftsman House Founded on the California Mission Style," *Craftsman Homes*, New York, 1909, 9 and 11.

[11] Most writers, and many professionals, interchangably used the terms *cement, Portland cement, concrete*, and sometimes *plaster*. Cement was employed most often as an incorrect catch-all term. Designers also used *staff* and *cement-plaster* when referring to stucco.

[12] Tres, "Mission of San Carlos del Carmelo, Cal.," *CABN*, June 1891, 64; E. Henrotin, "The Great Congresses at the World's Fair," *Cosmopolitan*, March 1893, 629.

[13] P. B. Wright, "The Great Exhibition Reviewed, IV," *AABN*, October 28, 1893, 48.

[14] M. Schuyler, "State Buildings at the World's Fair," *Architectural Record*, July-September 1893, 61-62.

[15] C. F. Lummis, "The Lesson of the Adobe," *Land of Sunshine*, March 1895, 65-67; California Portland Cement Company, *Handbook of Useful Information for Cement Users*, Los Angeles, 1899, 15 [Bancroft]; Cleveland Hydraulic-Press Brick Company, *Early Religious Architecture of America*, Cleveland, 1898 [Bancroft].

[16] R. L. Humphrey, "The Collective Portland Cement Exhibit," *Portland Cement Association Bulletin*, St. Louis, 1904, 4 [University of California, Berkeley and Los Angeles].

[17] Ibid., 6-7; also *Album of Photos from Louisiana Purchase Exposition*, St. Louis, 1904 [Huntington]. F.M. Mann, "Architecture at the Exposition," *AABN*, July 2, 1904, 5.

[18] E. S. Larned, "Description of the Concrete Residence at Port Antonio, Jamaica Island," *Cement Age*, June 1905, 6; C. DeKay, "Villas All Concrete," *Architectural Record*, February 1905, 85-100; W. E. Dennison, "Tile Roofs," *AE*, December 1905, 65-66; "A Tile-Concrete Roof," *Cement Age*, April 1907, 248-49.

[19] W. L. Price, "The Possibilities of Concrete Construction from the Standpoint of Utility and Art," *Portland Cement Association Bulletin*, Philadelphia, c.1906 [University of California, Berkeley and Los Angeles]. Also published in *AABN*, April 7, 1906, 119-120. *American Builders Review* published a similar argument in its issue of July 1906.

[20] In a sense, reinforced concrete buildings proved themselves in the San Francisco earthquake of April 1906. While brick and wood failed, concrete withstood tremendous seismic shock and provided superior fire protection for steel structural members.

[21] D. Lay, "The Use of Concrete for Cottage Building," *Cement Age*, April 1907, 250, 252.

[22] A. O. Elzner, "The Artistic Treatment of Concrete," *AABN*, May 4, 1907, 181. (Also published in *Engineering Record*, January 12, 1907, and *ABR*, February 1907.) W. G. Mitchell, "The Artistic Impression of Reinforced Concrete," *AE*, June 1907, 75, and, A. O. Elzner, "The Artistic Expression of Concrete," *IANR*, November 1907, 54.

[23] A. D. F. Hamlin, "The Architectural Problem of Concrete," *AABN*, May 4, 1907, 163.

[24] I. K. Pond, "Concrete Architecture," *IANR*, November 1907, 50-51.

[25] S. Coates, "The Use of Portland Cement for Modern Dwellings," *House and Garden*, September 1907, 104-06. In *Craftsman*: U. N. Hopkins, "Plaster Houses in the Southwest," July 1908, 425; "Concrete Construction: Its Possibilities," April 1913, 96-100; "Cement: A Building Material," April 1913, 123.

[26] In *AE*: C. F. Whittlesey, "Reinforced Concrete Construction—Why I Believe in It," March 1908, 35-57; A. O. Elzner, "The Artistic Expression of Concrete," July 1908, 41; C. W. Whitney, "Ransome Construction in California," April 1908, between 48 and 49. M. Schuyler, "Round About Los Angeles," *Architectural Record*, December 1908, 438-39; R. Moulthrop, "Opportunity for Original and Artistic Design in Concrete," *Cement Age*, January 1910, 17.

[27] *Cement Age* published Mission Revival designs from the East Coast prior to featuring ones from California. See *Cement Age*, June and July 1907 and May and July 1908.

[28] In *Cement Age*: "An Economical and Picturesque Concrete House," November 1908, 349; H. F. Stoll, "Novel Uses of Concrete in One of California's Largest Wine Plants," July 1910, 5-11; F. W. Jones, "Concrete Features of the State Normal School at San Jose, California," September 1910, 147-50; "A California Hotel of Reinforced Concrete," Ibid., 144. O. Morgan, "A Tribute to Cement," *AE*, December 1909, 99.

[29] *Concrete Country Residences* [California State Library, Sacramento]. Thanks go to John W. Snyder for locating this volume. See also Atlas Portland Cement Company, *Concrete in Railroad Construction*, New York, 1909 [Stanford].

[30] H. H. Saylor, *Distinctive Homes of Moderate Cost*, Philadelphia, 1911; C. E. White, *Successful Houses and How to Build Them*, New York, 1912; M. M. Sloan, *The Concrete House and Its Construction*, Philadelphia, 1912 [Stanford].

[31] In *AE*: Advertisements, November 1912, 142; December 1912, 177; March 1915, 3; May 1915, 3.

[32] The Mission Revival also appeared abroad. See P. Collins, *Concrete: The Vision of a New Architecture*, London, 1959, 90; S. W. Jacobs, *Problems of the 19th and 20th Centuries*, Princeton, 1963, 47; R. Koch, "American Influence Abroad, 1886 and Later," *Journal of the Society of Architectural Historians*, May 1959, 68-69.

[33] R. Vogel, *Das Amerikanische Haus*, Berlin, 1910, 264 [Library of Congress]. Thanks go to David Gebhard for pointing out that Vogel inaccurately attributed the Burrage House to Charles F. Whittlesey rather than to Charles Brigham.

[34] O. C. Hering, *Concrete and Stucco Houses*, New York, 1912, 104-05; I. K. Pond, "Concrete: A Medium of Aesthetic Expression," *AE*, April 1915, 61; I. K. Pond, "Concrete Housing," *Proceedings of National Conference on Concrete House Construction*, Chicago, 1920, 39 [Stanford].

[35] Pond, *Proceedings*, 41.

Chapter Six

A Victorian Dilemma

[1] S. Sloan, *Homestead Architecture,* Philadelphia, 1867, 25.

[2] In *CABN*: "Architectural Design," March 1, 1880, 27 and "Architecture and Building on the Pacific Coast," December 1880, 114.

[3] In *CABN*: "Departures from Old Styles," November 1881, 118; H. D. Mitchell, "Architecture in America," February 1882, 29; "What Next—Evolutions in Styles of Architecture," March 1882, 46.

[4] S. Power, "Pacific Houses and Homes, I," *Overland Monthly,* October 1883, 394.

[5] C. E. Norton, "The Lack of Old Homes in America," *Scribner's,* May 1889, 638.

[6] B. Ferre, "An American Style of Architecture," *Architectural Record,* July-September 1891, 39, 42.

[7] E. M. Henrotin, "The Great Congresses at the World's Fair," *Cosmopolitan,* March 1893, 629; A. H. Noll, "The Spanish Missions of the Pacific Coast," *AABN,* June 5, 1897, 75.

[8] J. Stewardson, "Architecture in America: A Forecast," *Lippincott's,* January 1896, 132, 134.

[9] F. S. Lamb, "Lessons from the Expositions," *Craftsman,* October 1902, 54.

[10] C. Collins, "The Possibilities of a Distinctive American Architecture," *AABN,* March 26, 1904, 99.

[11] Atlas Portland Cement Company, *Concrete in Railroad Construction,* New York, 1909 [Stanford]; Spier and Rohns, "Grand Trunk Railway System, Battle Creek, Michigan," *Western Architect,* December 1906; E. Brown, "Sources of Style in America," *ABR,* September 1906, 243; F. C. Brown, "English and Spanish Precedents in American Domestic Architecture," Ibid., 247.

[12] V. O. Wallingford, "A Type of Original American Architecture," *Architectural Record,* June 1906, 469.

[13] In *AE*: L.C. Mullgardt, "Our Interest In and Duties Toward Architecture," April 1908, 54 and "Mission Style Waning," June 1909, 99.

[14] G. Mitchell, "The Architecture of Mexico," *AE,* March 1909, 74.

[15] In *AE*: C.P. Weeks, "American Architecture," December 1909, 36 and C. Gilbert, "California Has a Distinct Type of Architecture," November 1909, 98.

[16] C. E. White, *Successful Houses and How to Build Them,* New York, 1912, 36-38; M. Mead, *Homes of Character,* New York, 1926; R. W. Sexton, *Spanish Influence on American Architecture and Decoration,* New York, 1927, 9ff, *passim* [Stanford]; F. Rey, "A Tribute to Mission Style," *AE,* October 1924, 77-78.

[17] I.J. Gill, "The Home of the Future," *AE,* May 1916, 85; A. S. C. Forbes, *Then and Now, 100 Landmarks within 50 Miles of Los Angeles, Civic Center,* n.p., 1939.

[18] J. G. Howard, "The Future of Architecture on the Pacific Coast," *AE,* May 1912, 46.

Bibliography

Although numerous books incorporate photographs of Mission Revival buildings, few address the history of the style. Those studies of note have been given with annotation below. Their listing is chronological, from least recently published to current. (All primary references are listed directly in chapter footnotes.)

McWilliams, Carey, *Southern California Country*, New York, 1946. Second edition reprinted as *Southern California: An Island on the Land*, Santa Barbara, 1973.

Excellent history of Southern California. Sections discussing *Ramona*, the growth of a mission legend, and the sociology of the 1880s boom are important for an understanding of the Mission Revival. Sections addressing the style itself lean towards a discussion of the Spanish Colonial.

Sanford, Trent E., *The Architecture of the Southwest*, New York, 1950.

A classic source of information for Southwestern architecture. Generalized discussion of the Mission, Pueblo, and Spanish Colonial Revivals. Like McWilliams, Sanford illustrates the reaction by historians of these years.

Kirker, Harold Clark, "California Architecture in the Nineteenth Century; A Social History," Dissertation, University of California, Berkeley, 1957.

First thorough study of nineteenth-century California architecture. Mission Revival section, with its brief analysis of the style's origins, is excellent. Bibliography especially useful.

Kirker, Harold Clark, *California's Architectural Frontier; Style and Tradition in the Nineteenth Century*, San Marino, 1960. Revised edition published in Santa Barbara, 1973.

Edited version of the 1957 dissertation. Remains the definitive study of California architecture of this period. Section on the Mission Revival unchanged in the 1960 and 1973 editions.

Gebhard, David, and Winter, Robert, *A Guide to Architecture in Southern California*, Los Angeles, 1965.

Guidebook to Southern California architecture, containing references to Mission Revival buildings.

Gebhard, David, "The Spanish Colonial Revival in Southern California (1895-1930)," *Journal of the Society of Architectural Historians*, May 1967, 131-147.

Definitive article on the Spanish Colonial. Discussion of the Mission Revival included.

Gebhard, David, *A Guide to Architecture in San Francisco and Northern California*, Santa Barbara, 1973. Second edition.

Guidebook to Northern California architecture, containing references to Mission Revival buildings.

Kirker, Harold Clark, "California Architecture and Its Relation to Contemporary Trends in Europe and America," *Essays and Assays; California History Reappraised*, San Francisco, 1973, 91-108.

Illuminates several points made in *California's Architectural Frontier*. Also serves as the thesis for the 1973 preface to *Frontier*. Historical analysis of the broader issues that were a part of the Mission Revival.

Gebhard, David, and Winter, Robert, *A Guide to Architecture in Los Angeles and Southern California*, Santa Barbara, 1977.

Guidebook to Southern California architecture, containing references to Mission Revival buildings. Includes stylistic definition in the glossary.

Gebhard, David, "Architectural Imagery, the Mission and California," *Harvard Architectural Review*, Spring 1980, 137-145.

Interpretive article addressing the issues of imagery and symbol in the Mission Revival. Evaluation of the style as a vernacular model for the Post-Moderns. Historical discussion drawn from author's 1967 article and from Weitze dissertation of 1978.

Index

This index includes references to captions and notes in cases where they contain pertinent factual material not found in the main text. Such references appear as follows: 132 fig. 85, *and* 146 n11, *respectively*. References in italics, such as *16 fig. 12,* refer to the photographs themselves, not to the accompanying captions. With few exceptions, buildings such as houses, hotels and depots are entered under the city of their location, with references also given under their architect or patron.